Crafting a Magical Life

Manifesting your Heart's Desire through Creative Projects

Crafting a Magical Life

Manifesting your Heart's Desire
through Creative Projects

Carol Holaday

FINDHORN PRESS

Published in 2009 by Findhorn Press, Scotland

ISBN 978-1-84409-161-4

Edited by Sandra Sedgbeer
Proofread by Shari Mueller
Cover and interior design by Damian Keenan
Printed in China

1 2 3 4 5 6 7 8 9 10 11 12 14 13 12 11 10 09

Published by
Findhorn Press
305a The Park, Findhorn
Forres IV36 3TE
Scotland, UK

Telephone
+44 (0)1309 690 582
Fax
+44 (0)131 777 2711

info@findhornpress.com
www.findhornpress.com

Acknowledgments

My deepest love and thanks to:

Sandie Sedgbeer, my best friend and mentor, who taught
and continues to teach me how to be a better writer.

My husband Chris for enthusiastically supporting me in
my art and writing endeavors (and everything else) and for
loving me through the creative process.

My daughter, Sarah, for helping me with crafts and photos.

Damian Keenan for a beautiful cover and for going above
and beyond the call of duty to bring the images and
illustrations in this book to life.

My friends Diana Disimone and Alex Williams, at the
Tree of Life store, for letting me try out all of my ideas in
their classes.

CONVERSION RATE

*For ease of use the Imperial/Metric
conversions have been rounded-off,
e.g. 1" = 25,4 mm to 1" = 25 mm.*

Contents

Introduction

ALL OF US yearn to have a great life. We aspire to feel healthy, live in a nice place, eat well, do work that we find fulfilling, enjoy financial security, and love and be loved. Some people think that you have to be born lucky in order to enjoy these things. And when these things don't happen they take it as proof that the best things in life are only available to the favored few. The truth is we all have the power to create anything and everything our heart longs for. The problem is that most of us simply do not know how to focus our attention in a way that has actually been proven to attract the things we desire.

I have to admit that I was the poster child for creating the worst possible outcomes for myself. I fretted about money, agonized about my love life, worried about my children, obsessed about my body, and felt imprisoned by my job. Like a hamster in a wheel, my thoughts constantly cycled with negative scenarios and accompanying inner dialogue that reflected my fears of being downtrodden, mistreated, overlooked and impotent to do anything to improve my lot in life.

And what did I get for all that fretting?

My financial situation spiraled down. My love life was a mess. My children continued to be a source of concern, and my worries about my job escalated to the point where I dreaded going to work each day.

So I went through life feeling angry and resentful, convinced that the world was harsh and unfair. It wasn't until I was in my late thirties that I began to understand – and was shocked to discover – that my outer world was simply reflecting back to me all of the pictures of the doom and gloom I had been creating in my mind.

Boy did that bring me up short; to think that all the time I was bemoaning my fate I was actually designing it! It's not the world that is unfair, rather, it's how we create it to be in our mind that's unfair. By the time this epiphany struck me, my children had become an exhausting chore rather than the joy they should have been, my husband seemed distant and unapproachable, my mother had become a constant and vicious critic, and my mental state was tenuous at best. Life had reached a breaking point and there seemed no easy way to fix it.

Once I recognized what I had unwittingly been creating I knew that only I could change it. I started seeking out people who seemed to be successful and positive in an attempt to figure out what it was they were doing to make it so. When I compared their life to mine – their ways of being and doing to my own – I instantly became aware of deep feelings of discomfort within myself. I felt terribly intimidated by them and my feelings of inadequacy made me pull back from them. I thought they had something that I could never aspire to: confidence, knowledge and their absolute belief in their ability to manifest and accomplish whatever they set out to do. How come they had it and I didn't? What gave them that confidence and self-assurance? What set them apart from me?

In an effort to answer these questions and find the key to success I turned to my close friend, Sandie, who'd written a book on this very subject.

What I learned from her and from reading dozens of books on manifestation, metaphysics, and the art of co-creation set me on a path of self-discovery. The most important thing I learned was that when we focus our minds on all the things we don't want in our life we create more of what we don't want in our life. The secret to manifestation is to focus our energy on what we DO want. In other words, don't create pictures of the fat body, the tiresome mother, the boisterous uncooperative children, the critical and demanding husband, because all that does is invest energy in what is. Instead, what we need to do is change the pictures from negative to positive, and use the powers of our imagination – like an artist – to start drawing pictures of how we want things to be.

I started to imagine the children being cooperative, happy and eager to be helpful. I created scenarios in my mind where my husband and I communicated in a positive and supporting way, and imagined my mother praising me for being such a good daughter, wife and mother. Things didn't change overnight. But over time my mind automatically found different ways to say and see things. There is a saying that energy flows where our attention goes and it is true.

I have to admit that retraining my mind this way was a bit like retraining a dog not to get up on the sofa after he has slept on it most of his doggy life. Those negative thoughts would sneak in when I was distracted, just like a naughty dog sneaking up on the sofa when its master is away. It took time and effort but I kept at it, redirecting my thoughts away from the negative and towards the positive. Over time, lo and behold, my life did indeed change for the better.

I drew up a list of all the things I wanted in my life and I looked for ways to create them. I scoured magazines for pictures that represented what I wanted: a new job, more money, a harmonious love life. I cut them out and made a manifestation map or wish picture, so that I had a visual representation that I could look at to keep my mind focused on all the positive things I wanted to create. I took a tip from feng shui and hung my manifestation map in my future corner to remind me of all the things I intended to create for myself. Every time I walked past it I sent it love and imagined what it would be like when all these wonderful things came to pass, and good things began to happen more and more in my life.

Creation is a powerful thing. Everything in existence first began as a thought. The chair you are sitting on right now first began as an idea in the mind of a designer. Whatever it is you want to create first begins with your thought. By investing your energy in your creation, you are giving life to that creation through a huge concentration of power born of your desire. It is the sheer force of that energy that creates the magic. This is why talismans, amulets, and other power objects have traditionally been held as possessing potent magical properties. It is not the object itself, but rather the energy that goes into creating it, and the belief in its potency, it that is the source of the power.

WHEN I STARTED working seriously with tools, prayers and ritual to manifest my desires, I wanted to try out just about everything I read or learned about. I followed instructions to the letter but found that sometimes this just didn't feel right to me. I experimented with different ways of doing things and started using my own imagination and being inventive. I created wands, designed runes, rolled candles, constructed wish pictures, and more, and they all seemed to work better for me when I did them my way.

Because I desire for the magical and spiritual crafts in this book to appeal to and work for as many different people as possible I have attempted to present them in a way that is open to individual interpretation. I encourage you to experiment for yourself, take from them what works for you, feel free to alter whatever you need to make them even better, and leave aside the ones that do not resonate or appeal to you. After all, I wrote this book for you and want you to use it in a way that you find works best. And most of all, I hope you will have fun with this. You are a creator in your own right and this book represents a creator's tool box or toy box, depending on your perspective.

So, I invite you to now gather together a few supplies, your imagination, and your desire and then invest a bit of time in the creation of your own beautiful objects and experiences to enrich your life and your environment. I can guarantee that, in addition to having more fun than you can possibly imagine, you'll soon be well on your way to crafting the magical life you desire and deserve to live.

CHAPTER 1

The Science of Magic

AHHH MAGIC! Just the mention of the word is sufficient to conjure up a variety of images in people's minds, from modern-day magicians performing on stage in Las Vegas, to early druids performing rituals within the circles of the ancient and mysterious monolithic stones at Avebury and Stonehenge, to Harry Potter weaving spells under the tutelage of Dumbledore at Hogwarts in the mega-popular book and movie franchise.

Regardless of whether we "believe" in magic or not, thoughts and images of the magical and mystical have fascinated us for millennia. The ancient Egyptians, Mesopotamians, Greeks, Romans, Celts and Danes believed in magic and employed it in their religious and esoteric practices through the use of mathematics, crystals, stones, runes, herbs, oils, rituals, evocations and chants. There was a time when oracles were consulted for their access to divine knowledge and tools of divination were widely used to discern future events as well as assist in making important decisions.

But magic and miracles aren't just confined to history or Harry Potter. As science is now proving, they are every bit as real as our physical bodies. For the truth is, even though we cannot yet ride around chasing the golden snitch on our own Nimbus 2000 brooms like Harry and his friends, we all have the potential to create magic that is every bit as powerful as anything we read about in books or see at the movies. That's because we all have access to the most powerful magical tool in the world: *the human mind*. It doesn't matter who we are or where we come from – rich or poor, old or young – we all have the ability to shape our lives and fashion our futures any way we want. And that, my friend, is what magic is all about.

According to the Merriam-Webster Dictionary the word "magic" comes from the Middle English term "magique" which simply means "the use of supernatural powers." And the term "supernatural" is defined as "relating to an order of existence beyond the visible and observable." These are certainly not scary or foreboding definitions and real magic isn't otherworldly, scary or foreboding, either. Real magic comes from within us and is activated by our concentrated thought about something we either want or do not want.

When I was a young girl my parents attended classes to learn Silva Mind Control techniques. It was the first time I had ever heard that what a person thinks can affect them. I remember that some of my parents' friends laughed at them for being "taken" by charlatans. Yet "somehow" my family seemed to always squeak out of any tight spots and turn around impossible situations, which I credit to their willingness to envision and experience positive outcomes. Jose Silva, as well as others such as Norman Vincent Peale who wrote *The Power of Positive Thinking* (first published in 1952) understood many years ago that the way a person chooses to think and act directly affects his or her experience of life. Their writings and techniques opened the doors to the idea that we all have power over our lives and our futures.

Since then scientists have discovered that our minds have far more power over our physical, mental, emotional and spiritual wellbeing than we ever imagined.

As scientists research how our conscious and subconscious minds, emotions, thoughts, beliefs, and brain wave states affect our bodies and the world around us, the mystery of magic has begun to unfold into the science of magic.

Researchers have been studying how the mind affects the body for years and each year we learn more about the amazing creative abilities of the human mind. Recently a Harvard psychologist, Ellen Langer, completed a study of two groups of hotel maids who believed they didn't exercise enough and were thus overweight and out of shape. When she convinced one group that they were actually getting plenty of healthy exercise their bodies changed, they lost weight, their blood pressures improved, and they had improved body fat ratios, even though they hadn't changed anything about their daily routine. The maids' thoughts and beliefs affected their body chemistry, which in turned prompted positive physical changes, even though they had not made any changes to their diet or exercise regime. Personally I quite like this idea!

You have probably heard of people walking over hot coals without being burned, and yogis lying on beds of nails or slowing their breathing and heart rates to the point of appearing to be dead. All of these amazing feats are accomplished purely by directing the mind in specific ways to control the body's reaction to the environment.

One example of how the mind can control the body is hypnosis. Hypnosis has been used in place of anesthesia for surgery and has proven helpful for many people who have skin disorders. There have been historical reports of individuals developing burn blisters after being placed under hypnosis and given the suggestion that a feather stroking their skin was actually a lit cigarette. The last example is quite graphic, and maybe even a bit scary, but it clearly illustrates the immense power our minds have over our bodies and how strongly what we believe can affect us.

Just about everyone has heard of doctors dispensing "sugar pills" to certain patients to make them believe they were getting real medicine. The amazing thing about this practice is that a good number of patients who take these inactive pills in the belief that they are real, actually do get better! Doctors call this the placebo effect and for many years have attributed it simply to the suggestibility of the patients. They also have discovered that if some patients take active or inactive pills or medications, thinking that they will produce harmful side effects, guess what? They experience harmful side effects! Doctors call this second effect the nocebo effect. Studies exploring the placebo and nocebo effects show that what we believe to be fact really can – and does – have an effect on our bodies and our health.

The recent development of fMRI technology and PET scans has helped researchers learn how our brain responds to the placebo effect. Tor Wager, an assistant professor of psychology at Columbia University, has used fMRI and PET scans to find out how the brain changes activity and chemistry when pain is present and also when a person thinks they have been given a powerful pain reducer. What he discovered is that the brain not only changes its response to pain but the brain chemistry also changes to reduce the pain. This study is very important because it is proof that the placebo effect is more than a mental response and clearly a physical one as well.

So how deep does this physical effect go? According to Dr. Bruce Lipton it goes all the way to the very nucleus – the DNA – of our cells themselves. Dr. Lipton's work on stem cells at Stanford University's School of Medicine has revealed that the ability of the mind to affect the body goes further than brain chemistry. Environment – including the beliefs and emotions of a person – can even alter their DNA. According to Lipton and others, this explains how some people – through their belief and positivity – can go into spontaneous remission and even experience miraculous healings of serious chronic genetic illnesses.

Did you know that your emotional wellbeing is more important in helping you live a successful and happy life than your IQ? At least that is what Daniel Goleman, author of the international bestsellers, *Emotional Intelligence* and *Social Intelligence* reports. Goleman explains that your ability to see how your emotions, thoughts and actions work together to affect yourself and others shows your level of emotional intelligence or EQ. Scientist and author Dr. Ervin Laszlo agrees and goes even further in his book, *Cosmos: A Co-creator's Guide to the Whole-World*, written with cosmologist, healer and psychic, Jude Currivan, Ph.D. Laszlo and Currivan propose that our mental and emotional "filters" affect this process causing us to be unable to become aware of anything we cannot imagine as reality. But if we are introduced to a new phenomenon – as my parents were with Silva Mind Control – and we begin to believe it really works, we will find ourselves experiencing the positive effects of it in our life.

Research into luck has consistently proven that those who believe themselves to be lucky and fortunate are statistically more inclined to be luckier and more fortunate than those who do not hold to such beliefs. Based on all I have learned about the science of magic, it stands to reason that if we choose to be happy and positive, we are, no matter whether we are a super genius or dumb as a rock, thus giving proof to the old adage "You are as happy as you choose to be." And one can take that further to say "You are as rich, successful, compassionate, friendly, etc. as you choose to be."

So, the positive thinkers have said it and the medical and psychological researchers are proving it to be true, over and over again: we are what we believe we are. This understanding has led many people to try to change their behavior or personal situations by adopting the use of affirmations, positive thinking or some other mind-shifting techniques. Sometimes these things work right away all on their own. Sometimes a combination of mind-focusing activities are required to help bring about a change and this has to do with the nature of the unconscious and conscious mind.

Your conscious and subconscious minds are magical co-creators.

Your conscious mind is responsible for logic and reason and is the part of your mind that handles voluntary things like walking, talking, chewing your food, etc. Your subconscious mind takes care of involuntary actions like breathing, heartbeat and heart rate, to name a few. It is also the repository for your memories, emotions (both good and bad) and the beliefs you've created for yourself because of them. So you may work with your conscious mind, telling it what you want it to hear, only to find that things don't change right away because your unconscious mind isn't getting the message or may be in conflict with what you are attempting to do. Helping your conscious mind to communicate better with your unconscious mind is what magical rituals and practices do by helping you achieve altered brainwave states that allow for closer communication between the two. The creativity and healing that can be achieved through the deliberate use of brainwave frequencies can have a powerful and positive impact on both states of consciousness.

Brainwaves are created by the electrical form of communication that takes place between the neurons in your brain. These communications are called impulses. The varying levels of energy created by these electrical impulses can be measured in hertz (Hz) through the use of an electroencephalogram. Your brainwave activity indicates your state of mind based on the frequencies recorded at the moment. When you are sleepy, excited, anxious, or scared your brainwave frequencies change to reflect your state. You can even learn how to alter your brainwave patterns in order to place yourself in a better mental, physical or emotional situation.

There are four brainwave frequencies that run from deep sleep to extreme alertness and all of them have an effect on your ability to manifest what you want in life:

Beta – *between 12-32 Hz* – When we are wide-awake we emit beta brainwaves. It is in this state that we spend much of our day, working, thinking, solving problems and generating new ideas, as well as concentrating, and interacting with others. In this state, our hand-eye coordination is better and we are bright and alert. The beta state is one of action, which is a necessary part of co-creation. Beta brainwave training is sometimes used to help people with depression or Attention Deficit Disorder (ADD).

Alpha – *between 8-12 Hz* – Alpha brainwaves show deep relaxation on the verge of meditation. When we daydream we are in an alpha state and the link between our conscious and subconscious mind is strong. Our ability to visualize and use our imaginative power is increased. This is an excellent state for improving memory, accelerating learning, and using self-hypnosis and mental re-programming techniques. When we do ritual or rote activities that help us move into the alpha state, we are more receptive to messages and creative solutions from our unconscious mind. Alpha is a powerful state for attracting what we want to bring into our life.

Theta – *between 4-8 Hz* – Theta is the state of deep relaxation that hovers between awake and asleep. It is also the state we are in when we are dreaming or experiencing REM (rapid eye movement). It is in the theta state that we might experience the sensation that we are floating out of our body. This is the brainwave frequency for healing and behavior modification because this is the state that also enables us to access long term memories as well as old emotional baggage. Theta is the most likely state for spiritual breakthroughs, increased extrasensory abilities, creative inspirations and the ability to retain what we learn.

Delta – *between 1-4 Hz* – Delta frequencies occur when we are sound asleep and provide another connection to our subconscious. This is the brainwave state our body uses for regeneration and healing. In delta we don't dream. We are in a trance-like state through which our psychic awareness and intuitive abilities may send us information.

Babies and young children under the age of six spend the majority of their time in the delta or theta states. This means that they are highly susceptible to suggestion and programming. You might have heard the saying that children are like sponges and this is very true. Without higher states to help filter information, young children literally absorb it all: how to do things, the wonders of life around them, and all the unkind words, pronouncements and experiences they encounter as well. The negative information stored in your subconscious can play havoc with your life and your attempts to use your incredible magical mind to manifest what you want. One way that spiritual and magical practices can be helpful with this process is by aiding you in achieving an alpha or theta brainwave frequency, through which you can access your subconscious and begin to replace self-limiting beliefs with more resourceful ones. Another is by allowing you to create a physical product that acts as a mental and emotional "anchor" to remind you of all the good that you are choosing to bring into your life.

We work our own magic every single moment of every single day, whether we are aware of it or not.

The things you think about and the words you speak send vibrations out into the universe, which in turn matches them and sends them back to you in the form of objects, events, situations and states of being. This means that when your thoughts consistently turn to your most dearly held goals and dreams, you are more likely to start imagining them as if they were real, which in turn helps draw them to you.

So why don't you always just get what you wish would happen, you might ask? If you think back you may find your own examples as to why this happens. You may remember some time in your life when you really wanted something to happen and you imagined it and loved it and then your "evil twin" stepped into your mind to tell you all the reasons that you can't have it or don't deserve it, thus negating the positive thoughts you had just put into achieving a positive goal. I have always wanted to write a book. But every time I thought about how it would feel to be a published author I would immediately think of all the reasons it couldn't happen to me, thus I negated my creation. As I learned about the principles of manifesting, I also learned to stop myself when I had those negative thoughts and replay what I wanted to happen, thereby erasing the negative thoughts and images. I also used magical practices and crafts to help me access my alpha brainwaves to keep my intention concentrated in the direction I wanted to go. As a result you are holding my book in your hands and reading these words right now.

Choosing components and hand-crafting your own personal magical items eases you into the powerful and contemplative alpha state, allowing you to experience high levels of creative energy which can also flow from your mind into the tools, enhancing their power many times over. Moreover, in addition to imbuing your magical items with your mind's energy, the focus required when crafting your own tools in this manner, also sends out powerful vibrations to the universe letting it know what you want to attract into your life. Spending time in meditation, imagining all the sights, sounds, smells, and physical sensations of having what you desire, also moves you more deeply into the theta brainwave state where you are able to send your subconscious mind new and more positive messages to overwrite any old belief systems that may have been holding you back from achieving your dreams.

Even of you do not believe yourself to be very creative or artistic, making your own powerful magical tools is easier than you might think.

Some of the crafts described in this book may be appealing to you and some may not resonate with you at all. So choose one or several which "feel right" and work at creating them for yourself, in your own way, using your own ideas of what works best for you.

By employing the science of magic, and your own creative process, you can take charge of your own destiny and achieve your heart's desires. Love, luck, health and happiness are available to everyone, including you. All you have to do is *believe* in the power of your own mind and start crafting the life and the future you long for.

CHAPTER 2

Divining Pendulum

WHEN I NEED to make a decision fast and am not sure what to do, I reach in my purse, pull out my favorite pendulum, and start asking questions. My 'purse pendulum' is tiny, with only a 3" (75 mm) chain, so that I can use it under any circumstance, even in situations where I would prefer not to draw attention to myself. I have seen people in stores and restaurants using small pendulums to make decisions about a possible purchase or dowsing the menu or their food to be sure it is the right thing for their body. Over time, I have become very adept at using the pendulum, and because I use it frequently, my success rate is very high.

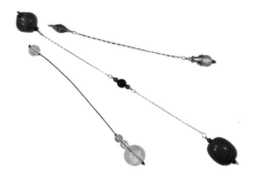

Some people think that pendulums are occult tools but they are actually very practical instruments used daily by people in all walks of life and for all kinds of purposes that you might not expect. There are a number of large companies in the oil, water and diamond industries that pay hefty fees to have professional dowsers utilizing pendulums or dowsing rods to locate gold, seams of oil, underground aquifers filled with fresh water, profitable minerals and other valuable resources. I have a close family member who works in the business of locating underground lines, tanks and other hidden objects for environmental remediation. Though he uses some very high tech equipment on his job, I have seen him double check his findings with simple copper dowsing rods or his favorite crystal pendulum.

Dowsing is an ancient art whose origins are lost in prehistory, though evidence of the existence of dowsing in early cultures has been found around the world. Ancient North African cave paintings dating back eight thousand years show a dowser using a forked branch to locate water. Four-thousand-year-old drawings on temple walls in Egypt show people using dowsing tools, and excavations of ancient tombs have turned up dowsing pendulums.

In fact, dowsing was popular with just about every culture in antiquity. The famous Oracle of Delphi was known to use dowsing tools and the sacred Urim and Thumin used by Old Testament Jewish priests are believed to have been dowsing devices. Dowsing is frequently mentioned in the Old Testament of the Bible and was considered a common practice back then. In more recent times, dowsing became an underground art practiced and passed on in secrecy due to the condemnation of the Christian Church.

In the late 1800s interest in dowsing resurfaced. In the early 1900s, scientists like Albert Einstein began to experiment and work with dowsing tools, which gave dowsing devices a more legitimate appearance to the general public. By the mid-1900s, the use of dowsing rods and pendulums had again become a popular and effective way of locating objects and divining information and future events.

How Pendulums Work

A pendulum is similar to a magnet in that it is responsive to the positive and negative charges that emanate both from living things, as well as from inanimate objects.

The use of pendulums for healing and divination is based on energy fields rather than gravity. Utilizing a sensitive device, such as the pendulum, allows you to tap into and learn to interpret the different frequencies that pervade the atmosphere and the hidden signals that they carry. Rather than being a magical instrument, the pendulum simply acts as a communication device between your conscious mind and the deeper, hidden levels of your psyche known as your subconscious – or as some prefer to term it, your *superconscious* – mind, which knows the truth of everything. Normally your super-conscious and conscious minds are unable to communicate but the pendulum allows them to talk to each other through a simple language of swings and circles.

So the pendulum itself does not give you answers to your questions or find things for you, rather it provides a means for you to access, develop and externalize your very own natural inborn powers of intuition that you have always possessed but may not have always paid attention to. When you ask a question of the pendulum, you are really asking a question of your super-conscious intuitive mind, which then provides the energetic response to make the pendulum move in the direction that will indicate the answer that is tucked away inside your subconscious. The more you work with a pendulum the better you will become at accessing your intuitive self and receiving accurate answers.

Once you become adept with your pendulum you can use it for just about any purpose including:

- Solving your most pressing problems
- Making important decisions
- Finding hidden or mislaid objects
- Testing foods to determine if the ingredients are healthy for you to eat
- Discovering which vitamins or minerals you might be lacking
- Asking questions and receive answers about your health
- Determining which horses or lottery numbers are the most likely winners
- Receiving accurate answers to all your questions about luck, money, love, work, travel, business or career

Regardless of whether your questions are about family concerns, career issues, education, health problems, money matters or any other situation, as you become more skilled with your pendulum, your powers of decision-making will be enhanced and your pendulum will become an even more precise tool for receiving advice and choosing the best course of action.

Making Your Own Pendulum

Making a simple pendulum involves suspending a weighted item at the end of a cord or chain. Some people wear pendants that they can remove from their neck and use as a pendulum. Impromptu or simple pendulums have been made by suspending a needle on a thread or a wedding ring on a string. You can fashion one with cord and beads yourself. Just make sure that the cord you pick will fit through the holes in the beads you choose for your pendulum.

You will need:

- 1 large 12 mm to 15 mm bead of glass, metal, stone or wood (as long as it is heavy enough to weigh down the cord)

- 12" to 18" (30 to 45 cm) of heavy silk twist or thin satin cord
- 1-10 mm to 13 mm bead to use as a topper or handle
- 1-8 mm bead
- 1-6 mm bead
- Scissors
- Superglue

1. Tie a double knot to one end of the cord. If a double knot is not large enough to keep it from sliding through the hole in the bead, make it bigger until it supports the bead. Slide your largest bead onto the cord and tighten it down against the knot. Put a drop of superglue on the knot and allow it to dry before you trim away the excess cord.

2. Slide on the 8 mm bead and then the 6 mm bead and snug a knot down tight against the 6 mm bead. Dot the knot with glue and allow it to dry.

3. Leave a length of cord for the pendulum to swing from (the length is up to you) and tie a knot at the far end of that length, leaving several inches to attach the topper bead. Slide on the topper bead and snug several knots against the top of the bead. Dab both the bottom and top knots with glue and allow to dry before trimming away the excess cord.

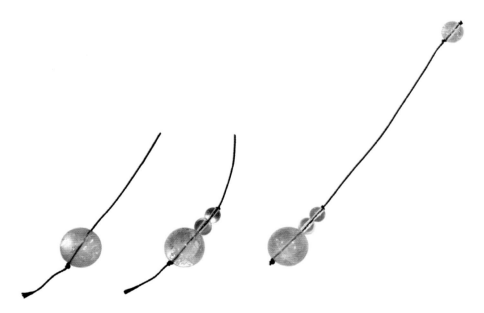

When your pendulum is completed you should cleanse it with sage or incense smoke or your breath and then sit with it in meditation and imagine how you will use it.

Beginning to Work with Your Pendulum

How a pendulum works is pretty simple. First you grasp the top of the chain or cord between your thumb and forefinger so that you can suspend it over the item to be dowsed without danger of touching anything. To establish your mind's connection to your pendulum, take a moment to imagine yourself deeply connected to the earth and clear of any negative energy. In order to learn which swings are 'yes', 'no' and 'maybe', start by asking, what the indicator of 'yes' is and waiting for the pendulum to respond. Next, ask what the indicator of 'no' is and await the pendulum's movement. You can also ask for an indicator of 'maybe' or 'answer unknown'.

Another method is to tell the pendulum which actions correspond to 'yes', 'no' and 'maybe'. Hold the pendulum and swing it one way and indicate this is 'yes'. Swing it another way and indicate this is 'no'. Swing it yet another way and indicate that this is 'maybe/unknown'. Once you have determined your pendulum's responses you are ready to ask questions.

Focus your mind's intention to establish connection with your super-conscious via the pendulum and be sure to speak commands out loud whenever it is possible. When you ask your question the super-conscious will send a signal to the brain to tell the arm which way to move the pendulum. The pendulum will then give a 'yes' or 'no' indication, and the movement is so imperceptible that it won't even seem that you could be moving it.

Questions that can be answered 'yes' or 'no' are ok though you may get even better results if you make a statement that will either be true, false, or as yet unknown. Statements that the pendulum can swing to in order to show agreement or disagreement are a very good way to get clear results, as questions imply a desired response. For example rather than asking, "Will I go to work for (name) company?" it is better to state, "I will go to work for (name) company." Be sure to use only one query per question. The more you practice the more adept you will become and the easier you'll find it to work with your pendulum.

It's important to be clear and grounded and to state your intent to have "the TRUTH above all else." It is also important to bear in mind that a pendulum can only ever give you the truth as it is in that moment. A day or week down the road things can change, so your pendulum might have different answers for you at that time. Thus, with important issues it is a good idea to check in regularly with your pendulum to see if there is a shift or change in the situation.

Also, when you first start working with a pendulum the swings may not be very big. So, when you pick up your pendulum and give intent to have honest responses, stop and take several deep breaths and relax your body before you start. You will find that the more you relax, the larger and more defined the swings will become.

Special Pendulum Grids

Using grids with a pendulum can be highly useful. You can make a simple grid on paper that shows specific directions for 'yes', 'no' and 'maybe'. Then hold the pendulum over the grid after you ask the question and see which indicated direction it follows.

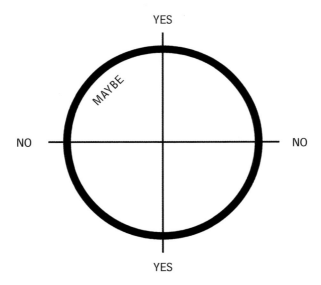

You can even create your own circular or semi-circular grids for ascertaining many things. Examples might be which vitamins your body needs or what colors will most benefit you emotionally at this time. The use of grids is limited only by your imagination. You can create grids for numbers, percentages, letters and more. Hold the pendulum over the grid and ask your question or make your statement, and then swing the pendulum in a circular motion. Watch to see the direction it begins to swing on the grid.

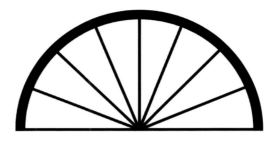

A similar technique may be used for receiving messages from a dictionary. First ask what page number. For this you can use a number grid. Then ask if the word is on the left side, and, based on the answer you get, work with that side of the page. Set your pendulum into its 'no' pattern and move your finger down the page until you get a 'yes' response.

If you are thinking of moving to or establishing a business in a new area of town or part of the country, draw a series of vertical and horizontal lines across a map of the area (if such lines are not already present). As with the dictionary page, set the pendulum to its 'no' response and move from square to square until you get a 'yes'. You may get more than one indication of 'yes', as there may be several good choices for you. Once you have thoroughly covered your map you can ask over each 'yes' square if it is the first or top choice, and move along until you have the squares ordered by highest to lowest benefit. Then you can fine-tune your search further by obtaining a list of streets and address numbers in the area of a particular square and dowse for the best address choices.

Finding Objects with a Pendulum

First choose an area or room and ask if the lost item is in that area. If it is then ask the pendulum to show you which direction you should head in from where you are standing. Then go to another area of the room and repeat the request for directions. Where the lines intersect is most likely where you will find the item. This type of dowsing is called triangulating, and it works well because you are searching for an item by starting at a number of outer points in a room or area. This increases the likelihood that you will locate the object you are looking for.

Clearing Negative Energy with a Pendulum

Clearing negative energy with a pendulum is really rather simple. You ask the guides, angels, etc. if you are allowed to clear the energy. If the answer is 'no' then you must respect this answer. If the answer is 'yes', simply set your pendulum into a spin and ask that the blockage be cleared. The pendulum should spin until the blocked energy has been released. You can always go back and ask again if the blockage is completely clear, and do more work if necessary. This technique can be used in areas of the home or property and also may be used on chakras and areas of the body.

Storing your Pendulum

Once you are finished using your pendulum you should wrap it in a dark cloth or place it in a dark lined pouch to protect it from any negative environmental influences. Also, since practicing with your pendulum causes it to become fine-tuned to your vibrations and create a special relationship between the two of you, you should keep your pendulum to yourself and not allow others to use it.

CHAPTER 3

Manifesting Map

VISUALIZATION has long been an important part of meditation and manifesting. Being able to picture something in your mind is helpful in focusing your intent towards making it come true. Some people are very adept at creating visual pictures in their minds and some find it more difficult to conjure these images up at will.

Whichever type of person you may be, the use of personally chosen visual images and text, viewed regularly and with intent, can help you to bring your heart's desires to life. I have used this technique myself with excellent results. But the first time I did it, I had no idea what a powerful tool it actually was and added images that I hadn't made specific, nor was I aware that I needed to spend time with my manifestation map.

Several years later I found my map tucked behind a chair and saw the "unassigned" images and instantly knew where those had come to fruition in my life. It wasn't the way I would have planned it but it was OK. Now, whenever I create a manifesting map, I take time to really think about what I want to make happen and make the images and text as clear and specific as possible. I also use the principles of feng shui and treat my map like a room or home, aligning my images and text with the areas of placement featured in the Bagua. The Bagua is a sectioned diagram used by feng shui practitioners to guide placement of objects in order to affect different areas or aspects of life.

The Bagua

WEALTH AND PROSPERITY Purples, Blues, Reds	FAME, FORTUNE, REPUTATION Reds, Oranges – FIRE ELEMENT	LOVE AND RELATIONSHIPS Pinks, Reds, White
FAMILY AND PHYSICAL HEALTH Greens, Stripes, Floral – WOOD ELEMENT	SPIRITUAL HEALTH AND WELLBEING Yellows, Earth Tones – EARTH ELEMENT	CHILDREN AND CREATIVITY White, Pastels – METAL ELEMENT
KNOWLEDGE AND WISDOM Blues, Greens	CAREER Black – WATER ELEMENT	TRAVEL AND HELPFUL PEOPLE Grays, Silver

You can create manifesting maps for a specific purpose or for a long term set of goals. For example, if you wanted a certain kind of new car you would look for as many images of the car as you can, along with text outlining all of its benefits and advantages. You'd find a picture of yourself and cut the head and shoulders out and fit yourself into the driver's seat of the car. In the money area of the Bagua you might put in a mock title showing that you own the car outright. In the 'helpful people and friends' corner, you might put pictures of your friends sitting in or gathered around your new car. In the 'family' area, love and romance section and other areas, you would find ways to depict yourself and the associated people or things involved with this particular vehicle. Any text (maybe written in colored markers or glitter pen), a date by which time you must have the car, appropriate crystals, or other things that visually stimulate you can be added to your manifesting map. Then you would keep the map in a private spot, where you could look at it several times a day, and imagine yourself enjoying your new car. You would also send light and love from your heart to the images on the map, letting the universe know that this is something you truly desire.

The Bagua is also helpful for creating a map of your long term goals, as you could place images and text representing all the things you want in each of the eight areas relating to the different areas of life such as home, career, future, relationships, etc. You could also use the colors associated with the areas of the Bagua to boost the energy of your manifestations. Wherever possible, include real images of yourself in the picture, as this increases the power of your visualization. Once it is finished place it somewhere that you're sure to see it often as a reminder of all that you wish to create in your life.

Making Your Own Manifesting Map

Creating your own manifesting map is fun and easy and doesn't require expensive supplies. All it takes is a little time and effort browsing through magazines or searching the Internet for pictorial representations of the things you wish to manifest in your life. After that, it's a simple matter of sitting down with all your pictures and choosing where to place each color, image, and piece of text.

You will need:

- One 12" x 12" (30 x 30 cm) square of white cardboard, illustration board, or foam core board
- One 2" to 3" (5 x 7 cm) picture or printout of the Earth (to ground your wishes into the real world) that you can cut out and glue to your manifesting map
- Pictures and words cut out from newspapers, magazines or printed on your computer

- Personal photographs that you can use to cut out faces or bodies of family, friends and pets
- Colored pencils, pens and markers
- Ruler
- Glue stick for paper items and or household cement for charms, crystals, etc.
- Crystals, oils, glitter, anything that will help you put the highest focus on your manifestation

Bagua Map

1. On your square of illustration board use a ruler or yardstick to draw lines from corner to corner diagonally and also from the centers of the top to bottom and from side to side to create a grid.

2. Glue your picture of the Earth in the very center of the board, where the lines converge. The Earth is the source of all of the things you want to bring into your life, and placing an image of the Earth in the center of your manifesting map provides a focus for your intention and a reminder that you are grounding your dreams into reality.

3. Begin gluing pictures and text into the areas on the board that correspond to the appropriate areas of the Bagua. Use your imagination to add other visually stimulating items such as crystals, charms, rune symbols, glitter, etc. Oils may be added, if you wish, but use them sparingly so as not to damage other elements on the map. Use the image of the Bagua, shown earlier, to help you.

Working with Your Manifesting Map

Once you feel you have your board completed, cleanse and clear it with sage or incense smoke or with your breath. Then find a quiet spot and sit with your manifesting map. Look at each part of it and imagine already having the things you are depicting. See those things, feel them, touch them, smell them, taste them, as if they were already real. Imagine yourself in the very situations you are attracting and feel how wonderful it is to have those things in your life.

Once you have built your own energy up through your emotions and senses, begin to imagine that the lines on the grid are made of light and are pulsing with universal light energy, sending out your signals to the universe to be brought back to you in full. Imagine the lines extending forever in every direction including above and below your map. Then allow the light to grow even more, to extend outside the lines and to fill the map completely

When you feel you are ready say a short prayer or say something like:

> *"Let all these things that I call for,*
> *or something even better, come to pass*
> *with ease, grace, peace, joy and laughter.*
> *It is my intent that the manifestation of these*
> *things be in the highest good and harm none.*
> *And so it is.*
> *And so it is.*
> *And so it is.*
> *It is done."*

Place your activated manifesting grid in a spot where you will be able to see it each day but where it will not be seen or handled by others. Some people keep theirs in a special drawer at work or in a drawer or cabinet at home where it won't be disturbed. Find time as frequently as possible to look at your manifesting map and imagine enjoying all of the things depicted on it that you are attracting to you. Every time you pass by it, even during those times it is hidden from your view, send it light and love from your heart.

Keep an open mind and awareness of how things you have outlined in your manifesting map have come to pass. It is always a good idea to take stock every few months and note down any progress that has been made in each area. If one area of your map appears to need extra support you might even make another special map that focuses on that particular goal.

There is no limit to the number or types of manifesting maps you can create. Some people save their manifesting maps for years after they have completed their purpose, simply because they enjoyed them so much. Others prefer to burn or otherwise dismantle maps once they have successfully fulfilled their intention. I have been known to make little changes and adjustments to my maps along the way so that one map continues to be usable for a very long time. You can keep, change, or dispose of your manifesting maps in whatever way feels right to you.

CHAPTER 4

Power Prayer Beads

WHEN I WAS a young woman I was fascinated with the Catholics and their rosaries. I used to wonder how long it took to say all those prayers, and what it was all for. It wasn't until years later that I began to understand the power of the spoken word and the repeated reciting of prayerful words. There came a time when I was in great need of Divine assistance and I decided to try out the power of prayer beads. I spent hours choosing the beads for my manifesting strand and chose a central focal bead that spoke to me of growing good things. As I built my prayer beads, I recited a little prayer chant over and over to myself.

After I completed my manifesting prayer strand, I began working with it on a daily basis. Every morning I got out of bed, got my coffee, sat with my beads and prayed for a place to live that would fit my family's needs and our budget. I kept the repeated prayers short and very focused so that the prayer strand wouldn't become a tedious chore. What I realized the beads did was to keep my mind focused in the direction I wanted to go. Within just a few weeks the perfect place

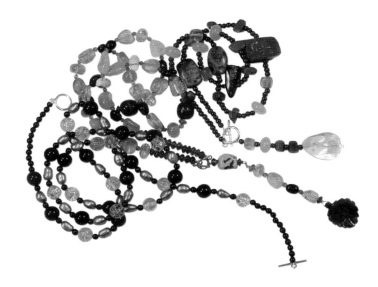

appeared in the area we wanted to live and at a price we could afford. Since then I have made several sets of beads for different purposes and have enjoyed the simple repetitive focus they provide.

Prayer beads appear to date far back into pre-history when ancient people crafted early beads from natural items they found around them. Archaeologists have found 30,000- year-old fossilized shells, bones and teeth that are believed to have been used as primitive bead talismans, which were worn or carried for luck in hunting and to indicate social status. Over time, beads grew to be so valuable that a number of ancient cultures began to use them as currency.

Beads were also items of spiritual significance and thus were carried as good luck talismans, like the sha sha, or luck luck beads of the ancient Egyptians (from 3200 B.C.). The Desert Mothers and Fathers, a third century culture, did not use prayer beads to count prayers. Instead they would find and carry a specific number of pebbles with them whenever they traveled, and would walk along, dropping a pebble and saying a prayer until all of the pebbles had been used. In this way they would insure that the correct number of prayers had been repeated. Another commonly used prayer accessory for those who could not ob-tain beads due to their cost or scarcity, was a length of twine or cord, which was knotted a prescribed number of times, so that each knot acted as a bead and indicated a specific prayer.

The ancient Chinese counting abacus may have been the original inspiration for stringing beads to count prayers. Hindus living in the eighth century have been given credit for being the first culture to adapt the purpose of the Chinese abacus to counting prayers on a string or strand of thread. One could say a prayer and slide a bead until the set number of prayers had been completed, much in the way the Desert Mothers and Fathers had dropped their prayer pebbles. The handy part was that the strand could be worn or carried for use at any time.

The word 'bead' originates from the Anglo-Saxon word, 'bede', meaning prayer. So, even the name gives testimony to the spiritual and religious connotation that beads have carried throughout the centuries. Prayer beads are now widely used around the world by a number of different religions. Many people make their own prayer beads from meaningful components and use them in personalized forms of spiritual practice.

Anyone can learn to make a set of serviceable prayer beads to suit their own religious or spiritual beliefs; to attract love, luck and prosperity; or to honor a specific deity, season, element, or planet, etc. Prayer beads can also take the form of bracelets, necklaces, altar decorations, wall hangings or even pocket talismans.

They can be fashioned from beads made of wood, bone, teeth, seeds, glass, crystal, gemstones, clay, flower petals and more. You can hand-make beads or obtain them from craft supply houses, online resources or your local bead shop. They can be strung on silk, tiger tail wire, satin cord, twine, sinew or floss, to name a few. Many prayer beads have a specially sized or shaped central focus bead or charm, which may also be hand-made or purchased. The only limitation in the construction of prayer beads is your ability to imagine what you want and then build it.

Prayer beads may be strung for any purpose you may have, celebrating a birth, honoring an ancestor, finding a nice car that you can afford, glorifying and worshipping, commemorating an event or even setting up a meditation. Your imagination is also the best tool for creating prayers to suit the purpose of the sets of prayer beads you make. You may find some examples in books or on the Internet that will fuel your imagination and creativity.

And if you want to enjoy using them for weeks or months at a time you should keep the prayers short and simple. It will be easier to remember each different prayer and it will take less time to pray all of the prayers, which in turn will increase the likelihood that you will stick with your prayer bead ritual until you see results.

Making Your Own Prayer Bead Strand

To make your own prayer beads you will need to decide what it is you are going to pray for, what kinds of repeated prayers you will do, how many times they will be repeated, and in what order. Then pick beads of a size and shape that will allow you to remember which prayer you are saying with that particular bead. Next, you may choose a focal bead to start and/or end with. This bead is the focal point of the prayer and it should be one that is meaningful to you. You may want to incorporate the meanings of colors, specific crystals and stones or the meanings of symbols (for charms) as you choose the elements for your prayer strand.

You will need:

- Beads in your chosen numbers, types and colors (keep bead holes similar in size)
- Special focal beads or charms if desired
- Cord or wire for stringing (appropriately sized to go through the bead holes)
- Scissors or wire nips depending on your stringing material
- Crimps and flat nosed pliers for tiger tail wire

- Superglue and scissorsif you are using knotted cord
- Desired type of necklace closure
- Soft plush piece of cloth or beading board to lay the beads on, in stringing order

1. On the plush fabric or beading board, lay out your beads, focal beads and charms in the order in which they will be strung, including necklace closures (claps and ring), crimps and the drop sections. When they are laid out they should represent at least 18" to 20" (45 to 50 cm) of length. If shorter, then extra spacers should be added.

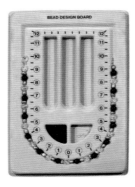

2. Loop one end of cord or tiger tail through one end of the necklace closure you have chosen.

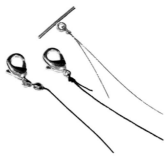

A. If you are using tiger tail you will slide a crimp over the two wires until it rests about 1/8" (3 mm) from the necklace closure. Leave about 1" (25 mm) of tiger tail beyond the crimp on one side and the rest of the length on the other. Use the flat nosed pliers to squish the crimp flat so that it traps both wires solidly.

B. If you are using a clamshell and cord, attach the clamshell loop to the necklace closure then attach the cord to the clamshell. Knot it several times, cut the excess away and apply a drop of superglue before using the pliers to close the clamshell.

C. If you are not using a clamshell, slip one end of the cord through one side of the necklace closure and tie a double or triple knot and then pull tightly. Put a drop of superglue on the knot to keep it from coming loose. Cut away the excess tail of cord after the superglue is thoroughly dry.

3. String your beads in the order in which you have laid them out, being extra careful that they truly are in the order you planned for them.

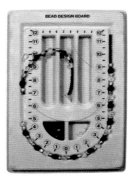

4. When all beads are strung you will attach the other half of the necklace closure to the end in the same way you did in step 2.

A. If you are using tiger tail, slide the crimp on the wire before you slide it through the other half of the necklace closure. Then slide the wire end back down through the crimp so that it catches the necklace closure in its loop. Pull the end of the tiger tail until it is at least 1/8" (3 mm) from the end bead and another 1/8" from the closure and then use the flat nosed pliers to squeeze the crimp flat. Cut away the excess wire tails from either end with the nips. Hint – if you can thread the extra tigertail back through several beads before you nip it you will strengthen the ends of your prayer strand.

B. If you are using a clamshell and cord, attach the clamshell loop to the necklace closure then attach the cord to the clamshell leaving 1/8" to 1/4"

(3 to 6 mm) loose cord so that the beads will slide. Knot the cord several times, cut the excess away and apply a drop of superglue before using the pliers to close the clamshell.

C. If you are not using a clamshell, simply slide the cord through the attachment to the necklace closure, tie several knots, apply a drop of glue and allow it to dry before trimming away the excess cord.

5. For prayer sets that have a hanging drop at the bottom:

A. For tiger tail or cord, use the technique described above to attach to the ring at the end of the necklace. For clamshell, attach the clamshell loop to the ring and knot the cord to the clamshell. Add a drop of glue and clamp the clamshell shut. If you are not using a clamshell, then knot the cord several times, apply a drop of glue and then trim any excess when dry.

B. String prescribed spacers and beads.

C. Loop through bottom charm and use above technique to secure. If the bottom piece is a bead you will finish in a slightly different way. For tiger tail, slide a crimp onto the wire below the bottom bead, add a very small bead or spacer and then slide back up through the crimp (and up through the beads above if it will fit through the holes) then squash the crimp flat and cut off excess tigertail. If you are using cord, you can either triple knot the cord at the bottom or tie a spacer bead to the bottom and thread the excess cord up through the bead above before trimming it away. When using cord, be sure to use that drop of superglue to secure it permanently.

After you are finished building your prayer beads you should cleanse them with incense or sage smoke or your breath and then sit in meditation with them before using them for prayer. Find a quiet time each day when you can sit with your beads and say the prayers you have written for them. Remember to keep them short enough so that you can remember each prayer as well as complete your recitations in a reasonable amount of time. Here are some sample prayer bead designs and prayers:

Thirteen Moons Prayer Beads

Just as we can rely on the sun rising and setting each day, so too are the phases of the moon a constant in our world. Some feel that the phases of the moon have predictable effects on matter and Spirit. This prayer set honors the phases of the moon and the energy that can be used for manifesting during each of its phases. This is an excellent set to use for a long term manifesting goal that may take a year or more to come to fruition. Frequently, this prayer bead set is made with large, round, white beads to represent the full moon; large, round, black beads to represent the new moon; and large, gray beads to represent the waxing and waning moons. You can be really creative with the spacer beads, making spacers shift

color from black to shades of gray to white following the waxing and waning of the moon. They can also simply be smaller beads of a neutral color.

You will need:

- 13 Full moon beads
- 13 Waning moon beads
- 13 New moon beads
- 13 Waxing moon beads
- 53 Spacer beads (or as many as you need to make it long enough to be wearable)
- Clasp and ring
- Appropriate cord (24"-30" / 60-75 cm)
- Superglue and scissors or crimps and pliers

Thirteen Moons Bead Prayers – Beads should be strung so that the prayers may be completed in the following order:

- Clasp (if you are using a bar and ring put the bar at this end, lobster claw clasp or spring ring claps goes at this end also)
- Full moon bead – *By the full moon's light may I enjoy full psychic attunement and may I see the fulfillment of my ideas, activities and commitments*
- Spacer – *Hail to the beauty and grace of the moon*
- Waning moon bead – *By the waning moon may I complete that which I have begun and let go of that which does not serve me*
- Spacer – *Hail to the beauty and grace of the moon*
- New moon bead – *By the new moon I contemplate all that I have accomplished and now plant the seeds of new ideas and actions that will come to fruition in the future.*
- Spacer – *Hail to the beauty and grace of the moon*
- Waxing moon bead – *By the waxing moon may that which I have set in motion begin to grow in abundance and move towards a positive completion*
- Spacer – *Hail to the beauty and grace of the moon*
[Use beads and spacers to repeat the above sequence twelve more times]

As you pray this set you can use the name for each moon if you wish to. You might also consider adding an extra bead to start and/or end with to declare a long term goal for the year.

Full Moons

Month	English Names	Native American Names
January	Old Moon	Wolf Moon
February	Wolf Moon	Snow Moon
March	Lenten Moon	Worm Moon
April	Egg Moon	Pink Moon
May	Milk Moon	Flower Moon
June	Flower Moon	Strawberry Moon
July	Hay Moon	Buck Moon
August	Grain Moon	Sturgeon Moon
September	Fruit Moon	Harvest Moon
October	Harvest Moon	Hunter's Moon
November	Hunter's Moon	Beaver Moon
December	Oak Moon	Cold Moon

Five Elements Prayer Beads

Many people enjoy using prayer beads to honor the world that surrounds us and supports our continued survival and comfort. The five elements, Earth, Air, Fire Water and Spirit are considered to be the stuff that makes up all matter on the planet in some form or fashion. When you choose beads for this set choose ones that, in your view, represent each of the elements. For example, if I were making this prayer bead set I might choose a green Malachite bead for Earth, a yellow Citrine bead for Air, a red Jasper bead for Fire, a blue Lapis Lazuli bead for Water and a clear Quartz bead for Spirit. I would then use smaller colored beads to represent the directions and pick a neutral color for my spacer beads.

You will need:

- 1 large Earth bead
- 1 large Air bead
- 1 large Fire bead
- 1 large Water bead
- 1 large Spirit bead or representative charm
- 4 North beads
- 4 East beads
- 4 South beads
- 4 West beads
- 22 or 44 spacer beads (or as many as you need to make it long enough to be wearable)
- Clasp and ring
- Appropriate cord (24"-30" / 60-75 cm)
- Superglue and scissors or crimps and pliers

Five Elements Bead Prayers – Beads should be strung so that the prayers may be completed in the following order:

- Clasp (if you are using a bar and ring put the bar at this end, lobster claw clasp or spring ring claps goes at this end also)
- Spacer(s)
- Earth bead – *I honor the mother Earth and direct my efforts towards preserving and improving her health and wellbeing*
- Spacer(s)
- North bead – *May I ground myself into my desired reality of health, endurance, prosperity, and abundance*
- Spacer(s)
- East bead – *May the winds of change bring me wisdom and knowledge, inspiration and awareness of my talents and abilities*
- Spacer(s)
- South bead – *May the creative fires within strengthen me, encourage me and light my way always*
- Spacer(s)
- West bead – *May I experience self-discovery and receive guidance through emotional balance and intuition*
- Spacer(s)

- Air bead – *I honor and appreciate the life-supporting qualities of Air and I direct my efforts towards preserving its pure nature*
- Spacer(s)
- North, East, South and West beads (with spacers in between)
- Spacer(s)
- Fire bead – *I honor the creative energy and power of Fire and I direct my efforts towards its creative use*
- Spacer(s)
- North, East, South and West beads (with spacers in between)
- Spacer(s)
- Water bead – *I honor the life-giving presence of Water and I direct my efforts towards restoring and preserving its purity*
- Spacer(s)
- North, East, South and West beads (with spacers in between)
- Spacer(s)
- Clasp Loop or ring (that forms the other half of the clasp)
- *Spirit Drop or dangle* (section below is to be attached to the large open loop or ring that is the other half of the necklace closure)
- Spacer(s)
- Spirit bead

Manifesting Prayer Beads

We all have a need to manifest something important at one time or another in our life; we simply need to invest the necessary time and focus to bring our desired item, event or state into being.

You will need:

- 4 Command beads – *beads that you feel represent the energy of commanding*
- 3 Invitation beads – *beads that you feel represent the energy of invitation*
- 3 Belief beads – *beads that you feel represent the energy of belief*
- 3 Readiness beads – *beads that you feel represent the energy of readiness*
- 3 Attraction beads – *beads that you feel represent the energy of attraction*
- 1 Affirmation bead – *beads that you feel represent the energy of affirmation*
- 3 Declaration beads – *beads that you feel represent the energy of declaration*
- 1 Special ending bead or charm that has personal meaning to you
- 22 or 44 neutrally colored spacer beads (or as many as you need to make it

long enough to be wearable)
- Clasp and ring
- Appropriate cord (24"-30" / 60-75 cm)
- Superglue and scissors or crimps and pliers

Manifesting Bead Prayers – Beads should be strung so that the prayers may be completed in the following order:

- Clasp (if you are using a bar and ring put the bar at this end, lobster claw clasp or spring ring claps goes at this end also)
- Spacer(s)
- Command bead – *(Beloved God/ Goddess/Creator/Deity/Universal Source), I call upon you to draw to me _____ or something better. May my creation become reality and in so becoming harm none.*
- Invitation Bead – *I AM willing to have good things come into my life.*
- *Spacer(s)*
- Belief Bead – *I am worthy of having good things happen to me.*
- Spacer(s)
- Readiness Bead – *I AM ready to receive those things I have asked for if they are for my highest and best good.*
- Spacer(s)
- Attraction Bead – *I draw to myself everything and everyone necessary to bring about my desired result and I give thanks for all that I have today.*

- Spacer(s)
  [Use beads and spacers to repeat the above sequence two more times.]
- Command Bead (fourth and final one)
- Spacer(s)
- Clasp Loop or ring (that forms the other half of the clasp)
- *Completion drop* (section below is to be attached to the large open loop or ring that is the other half of the necklace closure)
- Spacer(s)
- Affirmation Bead – *May all that I ask be brought about within the highest and best good of everyone concerned.*
- Declaration Bead – *And so it is.*
- Spacer(s)
- Declaration Bead – *And so it is.*
- Spacer(s)
- Declaration Bead – *And so it is.*
- Spacer(s)

Ending Bead or Charm – *Thank you. Thank you. Thank you. It is done/Amen.*

CHAPTER 5

Magical Travel Altar

THE USE OF the altar dates back beyond written history to a time when primitive peoples kept sacred places in which they held rituals to call for successful hunts or bountiful harvests. Evidence of altars can be seen in the earliest known dwellings as well as in many ancient stone circles and other early constructions. Personal altars of one kind or another have been found in the excavations of nearly every culture from even the earliest civilizations.

Today, many people choose to reserve a place in their home that is considered a special place of prayer and honor. Often these sacred places, or altars, will be decorated with items of significance to one's personal beliefs and spiritual practices. The sacred altars are then used for prayer and meditation or to manifest blessings of love, protection, prosperity, success and more.

Many altars will have individual or religious symbols of the five elements – Earth, Air, Fire, Water and Spirit – often represented by handmade or purchased items that hold some special significance to the person creating it. Crystals, shells, twigs, flowers, feathers and other natural objects are also favorite elemental representations for many altars, as well as personal wands or other tools.

On my altar I keep an amethyst cluster to represent the Earth, a feather for Air, a smudge stick for Fire, a pretty shell to honor Water, and a quartz crystal for Spirit. In addition, I have a beautiful bronze figure that is the focal point of my sacred space. I have seen some altars that are very elaborate with expensive silver chalices and gilded wands and others that contain only items from nature to represent the elements.

Your own altar should be functional, but it should also be a reflection of your personality and beliefs because you will be using it to generate energy to bring you luck, love, happiness, prosperity, health or any number of other wonderful things. Some of the best ritual tools are ones you are familiar with, such as candles, incense, a favorite cup, bowl or statuette. Unfortunately, it's not always easy or convenient to carry a pile of bulky altar items and personal tools when traveling away from home; apart from weight concerns, there is always the risk of losing some precious items or breaking them in transit.

I got the idea to make my own little travel altar when I was traveling to Mt. Shasta, California for a week-long seminar. I had to fly and wanted to take my altar with me, but there was no way to carry all of the items on the plane. I was feeling a bit frustrated about the situation when I suddenly had the idea to make a miniature version of my altar. So I quickly cut out a circular bit of cloth and drew a five-pointed star on it with a paint pen. Then I chose tumbled stones to represent the five elements. I folded the stones in the cloth and tied them with a ribbon. When I got to Mt. Shasta I found a twig that I pressed into service as a small wand. My travel altar worked so well I spent some time designing a bag that could double as an altar space after I got home. I still use my tumbled stones with my new and improved version.

Your portable travel altar should have the same basic qualities as a stationary altar, except that it should be small, easy to pack and carry with you, and the items inside should be sturdy and durable. To make a simple travel altar, cut a circle out of leather or fabric, draw or paint sacred symbols on the inside, and use items such as stones, twigs or dollhouse miniatures to represent the larger versions of sacred ritual objects and tools.

In order to imbue it with your own magical essence it is best if you decorate and personalize it yourself. Every bit of energy you put into the creation of your travel altar is energy that will continue to build and be available to you for regular spiritual practices or emergency situations that require quick action and energy while away from home.

Making Your Own Magical Travel Altar

You can make your own magical travel altar to take with you on business trips, holidays or keep in your car for any situation. Using leather or a tight-weave fabric (such as microfiber or soft mock-suede), you can fashion a portable personal altar that you can use for a lifetime. Be sure to choose a symbol or design that fits closely with your personal beliefs and comfort levels. A pentagram to represent the five elements is certainly not the only symbol that lends itself well to use in a travel altar. You can even make up your very own symbol or design that nobody but you knows the significance of.

You will need:

- Tightly woven fabric or soft leather square approximately 9" x 9" (23 x 23mm) (mock suede works really well for this project as it has a nice appearance)
- Pinking shears and/or sharp scissors
- Leather punch if using leather
- Tapestry needle if making a fabric bag and using cord
- Fabric dye markers or indelible Sharpie markers (fabric paints are not a good choice since they tend to crack with use)
- Sewing transfer paper
- Two 24" (61 cm) lengths of floss, thin ribbon, thin satin cord, or leather cord (adjust length up or down according to the size bag you are making)
- Small sturdy representations to carry inside of the completed bag

1. Lay out your leather or fabric with the inside facing up. Draw a circle using a protractor, or by tracing around a plate or saucer that is the desired size. If the fabric is light you can use a pencil. If it is dark you may want to use a piece of chalk to trace around the edge. Cut out fabric with pinking shears (to

prevent fraying) or soft leather with sharp scissors (though you may be able to use pinking shears on soft leather as well).

2. Using the sewing transfer paper, trace the symbol or design you have chosen onto the inside of the bag's fabric. Or you can create a stencil and use light sprays of household spray paint to stencil your design onto the inside of the bag (this second option is labor intensive). Be sure to mark spots for the holes. For leather you will use one hole and for fabric two holes, one above

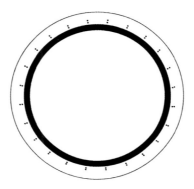

the other. There should be 24 holes for a leather bag or, for the fabric bag, 24 sets of two holes, one just above the other, spaced evenly around the edge of the bag. The sets of holes should be placed at least ½" to ¾" in from the edge. There must be an even number of holes in order for the drawstrings to work properly.

3. Use fabric dye pens or indelible markers to define your symbol and add personalized embellishments. Take care that you use a fairly light hand with them as they can bleed through to the outside of the bag. You might also want to adorn your travel altar with seed beads or other small and easily affixed items.

4. For the fabric bag, using a tapestry needle and light cord, stitch the outer ring of hole marks, starting from the outside of the bag on one side of the circle. Stitch in through one hole mark and out through the next hole mark, until you have made your way all around the circle and back to the same side. If you have done this correctly your cord will end up on the outside of the bag. Then repeat starting from the opposite side and following the in and out pattern of the inner ring of hole marks (just below the stitching points of the first ones), taking special care not to sew through the other cord. When finished, you should have two cord loops that enter and exit on opposite sides of the bag. If you are using leather you will punch single holes all the way around the circle. Then follow the above fabric instructions to thread the laces in and out of the holes. The difference is that you won't need a needle and you will use the same holes for the two laces instead of having two sets of holes.

5. Take the cord ends on either side, match that side's ends (maybe add a decorative bead) and knot them together so that you can pull them taut and tie a bow. When you open your travel altar it may not lay flat, but don't let that worry you. Having a cupped edge will protect the bag's contents from spilling when you lay it out (especially if it is opened on a surface that is not level, like a rock or your lap). Note – When you pull the cords you will have very long drawstrings. Do not cut them off as you will not be able to open the bag fully if you do. Simply tie them up in a large bow.

6. Some people like to use tiny miniatures, like tiny candlesticks or miniature table knives or chalice cups that can be found in dollhouse shops. Others prefer to use small tumbled stones as representations and tools. Still others enjoy using Sculpey Clay or baking clay to fashion thick rounded bead-like shapes to represent altar items. Use your imagination and keep in mind that

you will want the items to be as sturdy and unbreakable as possible since your altar bag may end up in places where it is subject to jostling or crushing.

After you finish crafting your altar be sure to cleanse it and all of its components with sage or incense smoke, or your breath. Then create and perform a small personal ritual using the altar to dedicate it to your use. Some symbols that may spark your imagination for use in your travel altar:

Some other travel altar symbol possibilities

| Celtic Knot | Tree of Life | Triskele |

| Pentagram | Chi Rho | Spiral |

| Triqueta | Cinquefoil | Ying Yang |

| Druid Awen | Ohm | Wheel of Life |

CHAPTER 6

Gemstone Amulet

IN MY PURSE I carry a petite polished amethyst elestial that contains an air bubble floating in a pocket of water just under the surface of the crystal. I consider this small item to be my good luck and protection amulet. When I take it out and hold it in my hand, my fingers curl around it perfectly and it feels very reassuring. My amulet stays tucked in a small satin bag that is black on the outside and purple on the inside. I feel like the black keeps negative energy away from it and the purple builds its spiritual power.

The first amulet I ever remember seeing was a small stone wolf encircled with beads that my friend's grandmother kept on her bedside table. She used to tell us that the figure chased away her bad dreams and kept her safe from evil spirits. We were never allowed to touch it but she would sometimes hold it up so that we could inspect it more closely. My friend and I viewed her grandmother's amulet with great respect and wondered at how anything so small as a stone could have such amazing powers.

Amulets and talismans are items of divination, protection and prosperity and have a rich history. The creation and use of the first known amulets was tied to the belief that magical power from the gods could be bestowed upon an object in order to protect the carrier or wearer from physical harm, promote fertility, provide victory over enemies or keep one safe from evil spirits. Ancient peoples believed that powerful spirits used magic for themselves as well as to assist mankind. Amulets were created as a way to confer specific magical powers of the spirits upon humans, depending on the need or purpose.

Archaeologists have found evidence of amulets that date as far back as 35,000 years ago. A good example of a prehistoric amulet is the Venus of Willendorf, a Paleolithic (25-22,000 B.C.) figure of Venus, which was discovered in lower Austria in 1908 by Josef Szombathy. I mention her because she is well known throughout the world as one of the earliest discovered fertility amulets. Ancient Babylonians, Sumerians and Assyrians were known for their use of figures shaped like animals or gods to bring protection, fertility and good fortune.

The Egyptians used dozens of amulets for a variety of purposes. Two of the most well known Egyptian amulets are the ankh, an ancient life and fertility symbol, and the scarab beetle, used for good luck and protection. Many ancient Hebrews used an amulet called the cheth (8th letter of the Hebrew alphabet) for protection, and the early Christians adopted the cross as a symbol of the power and protection of God.

Dogs, frogs, lions, birds, reptiles, winged beings, and cylindrical or conical seals were all used for specific magical purposes. Some were made of baked clay or fashioned from stone. Some, such as the cylinder and cone seals, were decorated with jewels and used as personal amulets as well as signature seals. In every culture and religion amulets found their way into the hands of the highest and the lowest, even when frowned upon by religious leaders. Carrying an amulet was a constant reminder of the power of the assistance of the gods.

Amulets were also popular tools for divining future events. Geometric forms and symbols representing the planets, and early runic alphabets served double-duty as items of divination. Rings are a form of amulet and the use of the ring for weddings is symbolic of the circle and the energy of eternity. Many people believed that wearing amulets with symbols used for divination made them even more powerful, and that belief continues among many today. Even now people wear a piece of jewelry with their astrological symbol or a rune for good luck or protection.

The use of crystals and gemstones in amulets is also an ancient practice. Cylinder and cone seals were often encrusted with gemstones and crystals to bring protection and good energy to the carrier. Stones such as agate, amethyst, topaz, jet, jasper, lapis lazuli and carnelian were available in the lands surrounding the Mediterranean and were frequently used in the fashioning of amulets. Lapis lazuli was believed to bestow the favor of the gods, quartz crystal brought wealth and prosperity, and carnelian was worn for potent protection from evil. Some crystals were carved in the shapes of various animals, which added to their energy, and some were made into pendants or beads to be worn or carried.

Carrying or wearing an amulet is a constant reminder that power has been put into play for your benefit. By choosing and focusing your intent through an amulet you send vibrations of what you want out into the universe where they are transformed and sent back to you. Creating your own amulet from crystals and stones is a powerful way to attract the energy of the things you desire. You can wear your amulet as a jewelry item, such as a bracelet or necklace, or you can create a drop that suspends from a belt loop, bra strap, or other clothing item.

Making a Gemstone Amulet

You will need:

- A variety of gemstone beads chosen for the specific purpose
- A fetish, or a number of them, if desired
- Bar, lobster claw, or spring ring clasp (two pieces)
- Tiger tail stringing wire, silk cord or other cord
- Crimps (for tiger tail) or Clamshell (for silk cord)
- Super glue
- Pliers
- Nippers for wire or scissors for cord

1. On a piece of plush fabric or a beading board, lay out your beads and fetishes in the order in which they will be strung, including necklace enclosures, crimps or clamshells. For a necklace, the layout should represent at least 16" to 18" (40 to 45 cm) of length so you may have to purchase and add a large number of spacer beads. Bracelets are usually 7"-8" (18-20 cm) in length and drops can be as long or as short as you feel comfortable with.

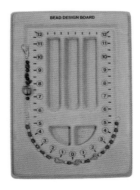

2. Loop one end of cord or tiger tail through one end of the necklace closure you have chosen.

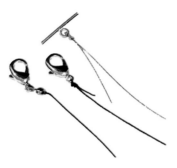

A. If you are using tiger tail you will slide a crimp over the two wires until it rests about 1/8" (3 mm) from the necklace closure. Leave about 1" (25 mm) of tiger tail beyond the crimp on one side and the rest of the length on the other. Use the flat nosed pliers to squish the crimp flat so that it traps both wires solidly.

B. If you are using a clamshell and cord, attach the clamshell loop to the necklace closure then attach the cord to the clamshell. Knot it several times, cut the excess away and apply a drop of superglue and use the pliers to close the clamshell.

C. If you are not using a clamshell, slip one end of the cord through one side of the necklace closure and tie a double or triple knot and then pull tightly. Put a drop of superglue on the knot to keep it from coming loose. Cut away the excess tail of cord after the superglue is thoroughly dry.

3. String your beads and/or fetishes in the order in which you have laid them out, being extra watchful that they truly are in the order you planned for them.

4. When all beads are strung you will attach the other half of the necklace closure to the end, just as you did in step 2.

   A. If you are using tiger tail you will slide the crimp on the wire before you slide it through the other half of the necklace enclosure. You will then slide the wire end back down through the crimp so that it catches the necklace closure in its loop. Pull the end of the tiger tail until it is at least 1/8" (3 mm) from the end bead and another 1/8" from the closure and use the flat nosed pliers to squeeze the crimp flat. Cut away the excess wire tails from either end with the nips.

   B. If you are using a clamshell and cord, attach the clamshell loop to the necklace closure then attach the cord to the clamshell leaving 1/8" to 1/4" (3 to 6 mm) loose cord so that the beads will slide. Knot the cord several times, cut the excess away and apply a drop of superglue before using the pliers to close the clamshell.

   C. If you are not using a clamshell, simply slide the cord through the attachment to the necklace closure, tie several knots, apply a drop of glue and allow it to dry before trimming away the excess cord.

5. If you are creating a single drop rather than a looped bracelet or necklace:

   A. Use the above described techniques to attach the tiger tail, clamshell or cord to a lobster claw or spring ring.

   B. String your beads from the top down.

   C. After you have strung your bottom bead, or fetish, for tiger tail slide a crimp onto the wire below the bottom bead, add very small bead or spacer, slide the wire back up through the crimp (and the bead if you can), and then squash the crimp flat. Then cut off the excess tigertail. If you are using cord you can either triple knot at the bottom or you can tie a small bead to the bottom and thread the excess cord up through the above bead before trimming it away. When using cord, do be sure to use that drop of superglue to secure it permanently.

Once your amulet is complete, cleanse it in sage, or incense smoke or with your own breath and then tune it to yourself by sitting with it in meditation and imagining it fulfilling its purpose. Wear or carry your amulet with you as a constant reminder that you are protected, guided and provided for.

Here are a couple of gemstone amulet ideas:

Scarab Amulet
(for protection and good luck)

You will need:

- Large obster claw or spring ring
- 5 lapis lazuli beads
- 3 malachite beads
- Scarab of lapis lazuli, malachite, quartz or other matching gemstone
- Tiger tail stringing wire, silk cord or other cord
- Crimps (for tiger tail) or Clamshell (for silk cord)
- Super glue
- Pliers
- Nippers for wire or scissors for cord

Attach the tiger tail or cord to the lobster claw or spring ring. String the beads starting with a lapis lazuli bead and alternating with the malachite beads until you end with a lapis bead. String the scarab bead. Tie off the drop using the instructions from step 5.C. above.

Native American Fetish Bracelet
(to bring energy of totem animals)

- You will need:

- 15-20 4 mm coral beads
- 15-20 4 mm turquoise beads
- Three fetish beads of your choice
- Bar, lobster claw, or ring clasp (two pieces)
- Tiger tail stringing wire, silk cord or other cord
- Crimps (for tiger tail) or Clamshell (for silk cord)
- Super glue
- Pliers
- Nippers for wire or scissors for cord

Lay out the beads so that they alternate between the coral and turquoise or create patterns with them. Fit the fetish beads into the planned strand where you want them to go. Attach the tiger tail or cord to the lobster claw or spring ring. String beads in the order you laid them out, paying attention to the length of the bracelet as it is strung. If it is too long, take a few beads out and if it is too short add a few beads in. When you are satisfied with the length and appearance, attach to the other half of the closure using the same technique you used to start it.

The above ideas are just to get you started thinking about what kind of amulet you would like to create. You can use the energy of crystal and gemstone beads as well as the energy of symbols and fetishes to create an amulet of your own design. The lists and keys in the back of this book may help you with your choices.

CHAPTER 7

Power Talismans

THE FIRST TIME I ever saw a talisman was when a friend of mine was locating something in his wallet and his paper talisman fell out onto the tabletop. I was immediately curious about what the little round paper disk with symbols on it was all about. My friend explained to me what a talisman was and then showed me how he had put symbols on the round paper that represented what he wanted to create in his life. His talisman was for protection from harm during travel. It made very good sense that he should have such a magical item as he had just returned from a tour of duty in Afghanistan.

My friend told me a story about his talisman, too. He said that one day he and three other soldiers were unfortunate enough to trigger a roadside bomb, which completely destroyed their vehicle. The explosion and ensuing fire should have killed them all; however, they all came through the incident with nothing more than minor scratches and bruises. He insisted that his talisman was instrumental in protecting him as well as his buddies, so he wouldn't consider going anywhere without it in his wallet. My friend's story was very intriguing and prompted me to conduct my own investigations into the power of talismans.

I discovered that talismans are magical objects comprised primarily of grouped symbols carefully chosen and charged with the very force the object is intended to represent and attract. Talismans are similar to amulets in that they are made to attract or protect. The difference is that amulets are more general in their energy while talismans have very specific purposes.

Talismans have been in use for centuries, particularly by esoteric societies and mystery schools. The symbols and languages have varied from one culture and time to the next, but the powerful belief, time, effort, and focused intent placed into their creation throughout history has made talismans very potent tools for attraction or protection.

Historically, talismans were made of metal and fashioned only on auspicious dates and at auspicious times. But specified metals aren't always available and most of us do not have the jewelry-making skills to create one out of metal anyway. The alternative to using metal is to use parchment paper and paint it with the color that corresponds to the type of metal one would normally have used.

The handmade talismans I have seen have been very complicated and intricately designed, often sporting Latin and Hebrew lettering, planetary symbols, geometric shapes and more. If you want to explore talismans in depth there are a number of excellent books dedicated strictly to their making and use, filled with symbols and talisman designs.

But even if you do not have the time to delve deeply into the talismanic arts you can create your own simple talismans for specific needs. It is even better if you can mix common talisman symbols with your own. Your own personally chosen and highly meaningful colors, shapes, symbols, words, and phrases will help to transfer and add energy to the talismans you make for yourself.

In addition, you can add to the energy by making your talisman on the day of the week or during the phase of the moon that is energetically most compatible to its purpose. The keys and charts provided at the back of the book may be helpful in planning construction times and in choosing some of the elements for your personal talisman.

Making a Parchment Paper Talisman

You will need:

- A piece of parchment paper at least 3" x 3" (75 x 75 mm) square
- A circular object, such as a jar lid, about 2" to 2-1/2" (5 to 6 cm) in diameter
- Pencil

- Scissors
- Ruler
- Colored pens or markers
- Planned symbols, letters and colors for your talisman

1. Use a pencil to trace around a circular object on your parchment paper. If you prefer, and you have one, you can use a protractor to make your circle.

2. Using the ruler and pencil, start at the bottom of your circle and lightly draw a triangle that points upward. Then lightly draw a triangle that points downward so that it overlaps the one pointing upward, creating a six-pointed star. You can even use your eraser to lightly erase line edges at intersections of the two triangles to make it look like they are woven together.

3. In the open spaces created by the triangles around the edge of the circle, place either dots or small symbols that are specifically related to the purpose of your talisman.

4. Using colored pens or markers, go over the interwoven triangles, and symbols/dots.

5. Cut the circle out of the parchment square.

6. Turn it over and draw symbols, words, or pictures that have specific meaning for you personally and are appropriate to the purpose of your talisman. Use pencil first and then ink or colored markers. Align the talisman to your energy by inscribing your name, initials, birth date, or birth sign on it.

Working With Your Talisman

When your talisman is complete, cleanse and clear it and then sit with it in meditation, imagining how it will work for you. Hold it and look at each symbol and imagine each symbol and word that you have placed upon it attracting precisely that thing for which you created it.

Many people carry their talismans on their person. Metal ones are often worn around the neck, but parchment paper ones are usually placed inside folded paper and carried in a wallet or purse.

A Sample Prosperity Talisman

This talisman is best prepared on Thursday, the day associated with Jupiter, the planet of success and confidence.

You will need:

- A piece of parchment paper at least 3" x 3" (75 x 75 mm) square
- A circular object, such as a jar lid, about 2" to 2-1/2" (5 to 6 cm) in diameter
- Pencil
- Scissors
- Ruler
- Colored pens or markers

1. Draw the circle and interlaced triangles lightly with a pencil.

2. Draw a '3' in the six outermost spaces and draw an '8' in the spaces that make up the points of the hexagram (star). Three is the number of creation and eight has to do with money management and the right use of power.

3. In the middle of the star, draw the symbol for money appropriate to your currency, i.e., $, £, €, etc.

4. Go over your light pencil drawings of the interlaced triangles and symbols in green ink. Allow to dry thoroughly and then cut the talisman from the parchment square.

5. Turn the talisman over and on the back draw the symbol of the planet Jupiter, since Jupiter has to do with confidence, vitality and success. Go over the pencil drawing with green ink and allow it to dry before cleansing and carrying.

The above talisman is a basic one that uses numerology and planetary symbols as well as monetary symbols. Creating it on a Thursday increases the energy of the intent you will be focusing into it. By making a talisman like this one and using your own symbols, words, etc. you will create a potent energetic tool to manifest whatever it is you most desire. You can use the zodiac, planet, lunar and planetary day charts and keys at the back of this book to help you choose the right day to fashion your talisman.

CHAPTER 8

Mystic Runes

The History of the Runes

BEFORE ANCIENT western Europeans had a real alphabet they used pictorial symbols, which they carved into stone. These pictographic symbols, thought to date back to the Bronze Age (around 1300 B.C.), have been found across Europe and particularly in the northern areas such as Scandinavia. These ancient pre-runic symbols represented the sun, the gods, people, body parts, weaponry, situations and virtues, through their design and communicated thoughts and ideas rather than words and phrases.

Many scholars believe that the ancient Germanic tribes (the Goths) who lived in the area north of the Black Sea developed a runic alphabet from these pre-runic symbols between 100 and 200 A.D. Artifacts of the time show that they didn't write in the traditional left to right word and sentence form that we are accustomed to today. They tended to use no spaces between letters, words or sentences. Instead the text would often run left to right and back again with an occasional x-like symbol or two to three points (similar to a colon) used to separate letters or groups of letters. Over time the runes have been refined into a set of glyphs made up of lines and they no longer resemble the objects they were originally intended to depict.

The word 'rune' is thought to have come from the old Nordic word, runa, which means mystery or secret. The oldest known runic alphabet is called the Elder Futhark, or Germanic Futhark, which is the alphabet most commonly used for divination today. Runes continued to be used as an alphabet through the 1600s when they were replaced by the early Latin alphabet.

Even after the Goths developed the runes into a written language, the symbolic nature of the letters remained important. This led to runes being used as a divination tool as well as a written alphabet. Often the runic letters were drawn on bits of leather or twig and would be cast upon a skin by a rune master to make decisions about hunts, harvests, marriages and other issues important to village life. They were also inscribed into personal items, weapons and religious objects in order to imbue them with the magical qualities associated with particular runes.

The practice of using runes for divination has been passed down to us throughout the centuries and the use of runes as a divination tool is still popular today. Nowadays runes are mass-produced on ceramic or glass discs and are stored in a soft fabric bag. A rune reading is usually conducted in a similar fashion to short Tarot spreads, but they can also be used with a casting cloth *(see Chap.16)*. I have one friend who swears by her runes, claiming they are more valuable to her than a horoscope or tarot cards could ever be. She says she pulls one rune out of her bag each and every morning and uses it to guide the direction of her thoughts and actions throughout the day.

I have several sets of runes that I fashioned myself and they each hold special meaning for me. There is one made of small polished watermelon tourmalines that I really love. The crystals are tiny and pink with green edges and I can hold the entire set in one hand. There is another made of carefully chosen egg shaped Botswana agate that I also enjoy using. But my favorite is one made from small flat pebbles that I picked up during my walks on the beach in Southern California. Over time I amassed quite a bag of small ocean-smoothed stones that I carefully sorted and sized until I had collected 25 pebbles of similar size and shape to craft my own set of rune stones. I then used a gold paint pen to draw one symbol on each of 24 runes, leaving the 25th rune blank. As I say, they are my favorites because of the energy that went into locating each stone, sorting through to pick just the right ones, and then carefully marking them for my own use. My pebble runes are like good friends with special messages just for me.

You can make your own set of runes to use for planning a day or getting some insight into a situation as easily as I did. They can be as simple or as complicated as you like, incised with a Dremel tool or painted with gold or silver paint. You could make them from ceramic or sculpey clay, slices of antler bone, small pieces of leather or round slices of a tree branch from your favorite wood.

Making Your Own Set of Pebble or Slice Runes

You will need:

- 25 smooth and somewhat flat pebbles or slices of similar size (have a few extra in case you make a mistake)
- An indelible ink pen or paint pen in a color that will show up on your stones
- A bag to keep them in once they are complete (instructions for bags are found in Chapter 20)

1. Wash your stones well and let them dry thoroughly before you begin. If you are using slices of wood or bone, sand the flat surfaces to make them smooth and then wash and dry them thoroughly.

2. Practice sketching the runes on a piece of paper so that you feel comfortable writing the symbols before you begin draw them on your stones or slices. The Elder Futhark Runes can be found in Chapter 22. On a sheet of paper, draw the runes in order so that you will have a guide to use for the next step.

3. Mark each stone with a rune and set it next to the rune on your master list so that you will be sure to make each one and not accidentally repeat one. Let the paint or ink dry completely and then examine them to decide if you need a second coat. If so, apply it and then let them dry overnight on the paper.

The Elder Futhark Runes

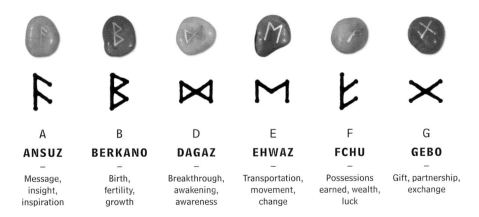

A	B	D	E	F	G
ANSUZ	**BERKANO**	**DAGAZ**	**EHWAZ**	**FCHU**	**GEBO**
–	–	–	–	–	–
Message, insight, inspiration	Birth, fertility, growth	Breakthrough, awakening, awareness	Transportation, movement, change	Possessions earned, wealth, luck	Gift, partnership, exchange

4. Find or create a bag in which you will store your new set of runes. See Chapter 20.

Once your rune set is complete and the paint has dried you can create your ceremony for dedicating them to your own use. A very simple ceremony would be to cleanse them in the smoke of incense or sage or blow upon them to cleanse them with your own breath. Then sit with them and imagine in your mind how you will be using them. Get a very vivid mental picture and when the picture is as complete as you can make it, imagine multiplying it by 25 and visualize the images settling into each rune. You will then be ready to use your runes.

There are a few different ways to use Rune for readings:

One Rune Reading

You can use the runes as a daily meditation tool or a daily guide by drawing one out of the bag every morning before you start your day. A one-rune drawing may also be handy for a very quick rune reading in response to a specific question. You may have to look up the meanings of each rune drawn until you become familiar with all of them. It is possible that the rune you pull will guide you to be extra cautious or will tell you that an opportunity will arise, or maybe that you will be connecting with someone from the past, etc. You can hold the energy of the rune you pull in your mind as you go about your daily activities and be aware of all the possibilities that it presents to you. In the event of a quick answer rune reading, think of the question, pull the rune and think about how its meaning may apply to the situation for which you are seeking an answer.

Three Rune Reading

When you need a bit more information or an overall view of a situation, you can use a three rune reading. Think of the situation and then pull your first rune and lay it before you face up. Then pull the second and lay it next to the first, and then pull the third rune and lay it down next to the second rune.

Rune 1 – Past events that affect your current situation
Rune 2 – The present situation or choice that must be made
Rune 3 – Result if the current situation goes unchanged (Fate)

Take a few moments to study the runes you have pulled in light of the information above. Look for connections between them and pay attention to your intuition while you are doing this. Your intuition can use the runes as a tool to guide you.

In Depth Rune Reading

This rune reading involves the use of 10 stones. Think of the question or situation and then pull the runes from the bag one at a time and lay them out like this:

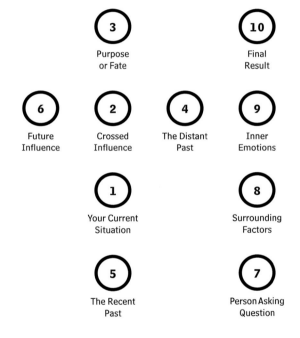

Casting Cloth

Think about the question or situation you wish to receive information about. Lay out your casting cloth on a floor, chair or table. Place your stones in the bag, gently shake them up and drop them out about 12" above the casting cloth. Alternatively, you can place them all into your palms and release them all at once onto the cloth. Then read the runes that are turned face up as they relate to the sections they have fallen in. Again, be open to the whisperings of your intuition while you are doing this kind of reading. (To create a casting cloth, see Chapter 16.)

CHAPTER 9

Magic Wands

JUST ABOUT EVERYONE has a little drawer or box for odds and ends picked up or saved from some special moment or event. Those items hold energy because they have been set aside as important to the person who collected them, which makes them perfect candidates for incorporating into a personal wand.

Wands and staffs are mentioned in many historical texts and have always been considered to be representations of power. The ancient Egyptian kings carried crooks representing their governance over the people. The Bible tells the story of Moses using a staff to part the Red Sea to allow the Israelites to escape the pharaoh. Around the world, various monarchs almost always have one or more jewel-encrusted scepters or staffs locked away in the royal treasury. In Great Britain, the King's Scepter with the Dove, the Queen's Scepter with the Cross (which holds the Great Star of Africa) and the Queen's Ivory Rod, are all valuable treasures used in coronations and ceremonies to indicate the power of the monarch and the protection of and governance over his or her subjects.

The Great Star of Africa (the Cullinan I diamond), which graces the Queen's Sceptre with the Cross, weighs more than 530 carats (106 g) and is the second largest cut diamond the world. The Sceptre with the Dove is a gold rod set with gems and diamonds topped with a white enamel dove, which symbolizes the

Holy Ghost. These two scepters are considered to be very sacred symbols of power and authority, as the Sceptre with the Cross is held in the right hand and the Sceptre with the Dove is held in the left at the moment the monarch is crowned.

But royalty are not the only ones entitled to wield a wand or staff of power. Anyone who wishes to have a personal representation of power can enjoy having and using their own personal wand. Wands and staffs can be purchased at local metaphysical shops, and you may find one that you truly love and will be happy to use or one that you could not possibly reproduce on your own. However, there is nothing quite as satisfying as creating your own wand or staff with special items that you have chosen yourself. Even when they are not as "pretty" as a store bought version they are filled with your very own energy and intent, which makes them powerful personal tools.

Over the years I have fashioned a number of wands and staffs. One of my very favorite wands is a simple piece of curly willow with a tiny quartz crystal embedded in the tip. My other favorite is one I created from sterling silver tubing and bezel, tipped with quartz crystals and encrusted with gemstones that I shaped and polished myself. I use each as I am guided to and feel bonded to both of them equally. Though I tend to use them for different purposes, each has its place in my life. I believe it likely that you will have a similar experience with the wands you create for yourself.

Choosing the Shaft for Your Wand

Wands may be made out of wood, metal, glass or other items, including crystals. Generally anything over four inches in length is considered long enough to be a wand. Great candidates for crystal wands include long thin calcite fingers, long quartz points, needle or sword selenite crystals, or any kind of long machine-shaped crystal or stone. Crystal wands may be used alone or may become a base upon which you can affix other crystals, cabochons, wire, sinew etc., to build a tool you can use in your own personal rituals and spiritual practices.

There are a number of excellent woods from which to build a wand. You might find one simply lying on the ground while on a hike or you may seek a branch of a specific wood that is meaningful to you. Natural sections of branch or driftwood are probably easiest to work with, though if you are ambitious and good with a knife or lathe you may shape your wand in your own way. If you are in search of a certain type of wood you may be able to locate what you want by checking with hardwood specialty companies.

If you are using metal for your wand shaft you may wish to consider a copper tube that you can obtain at your local hardware store. If you choose silver or gold you can obtain these from jewelry wholesale companies, but be prepared to pay a premium price for them. You can also take copper, silver or gold wire, or a combination of them and twist, braid or wrap to create a shaft that is thick enough and strong enough to support the crystals, stones or other items you wish to apply to it.

Some people like to use glass rods for wand building. It is nice to have the availability of colored glass to add the energy of colored light to a wand. Glass rods for wand making can be obtained from an art glass company. These are easily located via the telephone book or Internet.

You can use the color, metal, wood, and crystal keys in the back of this book to help you choose elements for your wand base as well as for the embellishments you will add to it.

The Process of Building Your Wand

As you work on your wand or staff you will want to view all of the components you use with respect as sacred items. Think of how the items you are adding will be of benefit to you and let your intuition guide you in their placement. Since building a wand may take more than one sitting, you should find some type of container or safe place to store your project in between work sessions.

You will need:

- Stick, glass or metal rod, or crystal as the base
- Small personal power items that may be affixed to the wand shaft
- Crystals, stones, beads, shells, small fetishes, silver or gold wire, sinew, leather or fabric
- E6000 or Household Goop adhesive
- Toothpicks
- Paper towels
- Protective cover for work surface (newspapers or plastic)
- Scissors for cutting fabric or leather
- Flat or needle-nosed pliers and wire nippers
- Household tape or clear packing tape
- A bowl of sand to hold wand upright while adhesive dries

1. Most people attach a crystal or stone to the end of their wand or staff. If you decide to do this, make sure that the crystal or item that you have picked is not too large or too small for your wand. If the crystal is too small, the wand body will overpower it visually. If it is too large, it will look out of balance and the stone or crystal may be difficult to affix and keep it attached. You can choose the best match by having several widths of wand base or several sizes of crystals/stones that you can lay together to see which combination works best for balance and visual appeal.

2. When you are ready to affix your tip to the wand, make sure that the ends to be glued together are clean and dry. If you are using wood you might try to hollow out the end a bit to support your crystal or stone better. Tear a strip of tape several inches long and catch the end on a counter or table edge where it can be grasped easily with one hand. Put a dab of adhesive on the end of the wand and on the bottom end of the crystal to be affixed. Place the ends together and hold them for a bit. It never hurts to have a second pair of hands

to hold your wand and crystal together while you remove excess glue with a toothpick and then wrap the joint with the strip of household tape. Then you will want to set it upright somewhere to dry and cure. A pot with sand or soil is perfect for this, or you may find some other way to prop it upright while the joint cures and dries. This could take a couple of hours. If you are planning to have a crystal or stone at each end of the wand you will repeat the process after the first end is fully dried and cured.

3. Once your main crystal is attached and the glue has cured you can use fabric or leather strips to cover the adhesive and protect the joint. If you are using tubing be sure that any crystals, herbs or vials of sacred water or oil will fit safely inside and then seal the bottom end. Now you can embellish your wand with the items you have collected: beads, cabochons and stones. When wrapping with wire it may be necessary to anchor the ends under a glued crystal or glue and wrap the ends with tape until they are dried and cured. It is important to remember that flatter stones or stones with one side that is flatter, fit better against the curve of the wand and are much easier to attach and much more comfortable to hold in the hand.

4. When your wand is finished you should consider using fabric or leather to fashion a protective bag or, better yet, look for a long, wooden box or hard case to place your wand in when you are not using it. This will protect it from exposure and cushion it from damage in between uses.

A note about air travel with your wand: New transportation safety laws could see your carefully created power item confiscated at the security screening check point, so you might think twice about taking it on the plane with you. Even if you put it in your carry-on luggage there is still a risk of it being lost or damaged. If you must have a wand with you on a trip choose something that you will enjoy using but not be devastated to lose and pack it carefully in your checked luggage. Or make a very small one that has no sharp crystals on it. Otherwise, if you really must have your best wand when you arrive at a distant location, consider shipping it in advance, carefully packaged and insured.

Dedicating Your New Wand

The time and effort you have put into its creation have already imbued your wand with a great deal of personal energy, but before you use it you will want to dedicate it to your personal use.

When you are ready to do this, create your own sacred space and use sage smoke or your own breath to clear and cleanse the entire instrument. Then sit quietly with your new tool. Imagine the history of the components you used, the life of a tree, the growth of a plant used for fabric fibers, the life of a cow, deer or other animal used for leather or sinew, the smelting of metal, etc. Your wand is made up of the gifts of the earth and fashioned by your hand. Take a moment to thank each and every element you used and the origin of that element. Then imagine yourself using your new wand for whatever purpose you have designed it. You may even wish to speak your thanks out loud and then speak your plan for its use out loud as well. Once the process is complete you may close your sacred space and begin to use your new wand or staff.

Each time you use your wand or staff you should handle it with respect. Keep it cleansed and cleared with your breath or by passing it through the smoke from sage or incense. Be especially sure to do this after you have used the wand or staff for healing purposes. If you take care of your wand and keep it protected when not in use you will be able to enjoy using it to put forth the power of your intent for many years to come.

CHAPTER 10

Crystal Grid

CRYSTALS AND MINERALS have inspired a sense of mystery and magic within many cultures for millennia. Early man used crystals and stones as practical implements to hunt, skin, tan, cut and sew, as well as spiritual objects in the form of tokens, talismans and amulets.

Historical texts of every culture show some use of crystals and stones for magical or religious purposes. Ancient Babylonian texts declare quartz crystal to be the stone of power. Old Testament Bible passages tell of the powerful Urim and Thummin as well as the twelve sacred stones of the high priest's breastplate that represent the tribes of Israel, which were used to divine God's will. The Egyptians used crystals and stones for health, protection and spiritual practice during life as well as on their journey to the afterlife.

In addition to being used as jewelry, amulets, and other spiritual or religious objects of power, crystals can also be used in patterned layouts for the purpose of invoking protection, healing or manifestation. You may have heard of the World Peace Crystal Grids that Reiki master William Rand has placed at the North and South poles and in Jerusalem. These grids were created so that Reiki energy could be transmitted to them to help balance the Earth's magnetic energy field and heal the planet.

Several years ago, I woke up one night after having a very powerful dream, feeling a sudden compulsion to create my own crystal grid in my backyard. I had no idea what prompted it, but once I was awake the compulsion took hold. Tip-toeing through the house so as not to wake my husband or children, I quietly carried my box of crystals outside. And in the light of the moon I carefully se-lected 33 crystals to use in creating my own crystal grid. I had no idea why I was prompted to use 33. I just knew that was the number that felt right. I meticu-lously measured and mapped out a circle that was twelve feet in diameter and placed 22 of them in the ground all around the perimeter, just like seeds, with their points facing straight up. Then I made a smaller, inner circle that was exactly six feet in diameter, and did the same using the remaining eleven crystals. In the center of the circle I placed a pebble to help me remember where the center of my grid was. Strangely enough, the center proved easy to find even without the pebble. I spent many a morning or evening in my circle, imagining lines of light shooting through the crystals and forming a cone of brilliance, which I would then visualize flowing into the ground. It was my way to send love to the Earth. I enjoyed this experience so much that I buried a second circle on a hill overlook-ing Lake Maxinkuckee in Indiana. Even now, though distance and years have separated me from both of those crystal grids, I can still access them in my mind and heart and I fully believe that they respond to my mental touch.

Since then I have created dozens of grids for many different purposes includ-ing protecting hearth and home, clearing and attracting energy, manifesting, and healing. The wonderful thing about crystal grids is that unless they are buried or the crystals are extremely large, they can be easily moved to new locations or reorganized or reassigned.

You don't have to go to the polar ice caps, or bury dozens of crystals in your back yard to find a way to use crystal grids for your own purposes. You simply need to hold your purpose in mind and then use your imagination to combine crystals and stones on a grid, according to your need.

Circular Grids

Crystal grids, similar to the ones I created, are practical and portable and are easy to create and use for a number of purposes. Different types of grids use different quantities of crystals. For example, a fairy grid usually incorporates 11 crystals and a medicine wheel grid (often used for health purposes) will be composed of eight outer crystals. Numerology seems to be important and you can consult the numerology page at the back of the book for the meanings and purposes of different numbers as you plan your own crystal grids. Circular grids are often aligned to physical north to take advantage of the magnetic energy of the poles. If for some reason you cannot or choose not to align your grid to the physical north, you can align it to the "north" section of your grid diagram. You might create a diagram similar to the one shown below on paper, or even on a cloth (using the steps described in the chapter on crystal casting cloths).

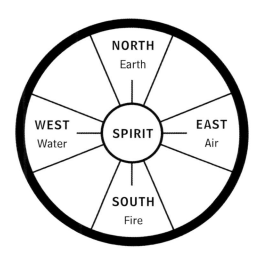

Using Circle Grids:
Moving Stagnant or Concentrated Energy

Sometimes an area of your home or office can feel uncomfortable due to an energy imbalance of some sort. Corners can often feel a bit stagnant because the energy is trapped in a space where it cannot flow. Sometimes, especially in an area where many people meet and work, the energy can feel concentrated, and uncomfortable. If you've ever felt uncomfortable after being in a large crowd, you probably experienced an overdose of heavy, concentrated energy caused by masses of people and their many conflicting thoughts and emotions.

You can use circle grids to clear an area of excess energy or to concentrate and move energy that is feeling stuffy and stagnant. If you don't want others to know what you are doing, you can do this unobtrusively with tiny crystals. To revitalize an energetically sluggish space, place a crystal grid in the area with your circle of crystals facing outward and imagine vital earth energy being drawn in through the central crystal to be sent out into the space through the smaller crystals. When you have a need to draw off excess energy, simply do the opposite; point the crystals inward toward the central crystal and imagine the energy being drawn through the ring of crystals into the central crystal and then from there into the Earth to be transformed and reused.

Using Circle Grids: Manifesting

If there is something that you particularly want to make happen, start by either writing down the desired outcome on a piece of paper, as if it already has happened, or locate a picture of what it is you want. Place the image or text in the center of your crystal diagram, under the central crystal, and point all of the circle crystals inward on your crystal grid. You might also add other crystals and stones that have energies that support your manifesting activity.

For example, if you want a specific job that has become available at your office, you could take the job posting and write your name across it. Then place it under the central crystal of your crystal diagram and point the circle of crystals inward. Next you might add to the diagram, in locations that feel right to you, a piece of citrine for personal power and good luck, a carnelian for enthusiasm and motivation, sodalite for clear thinking and unakite for cooperation and unity. Then you would sit near your crystal grid and imagine light emanating from the outer crystals, through the additional stones you have placed on the diagram, into the central crystal and from there into the job posting with your name on it.

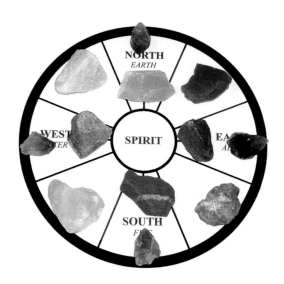

Every time you walk past the grid, even if it is just for a few seconds, imagine yourself performing successfully and happily in your new job and visualize the energy continuing to flow through the crystals. When you have manifested the job and are fully settled into it you can visualize the energy of the crystals closing down and then dismantle the grid. Be sure to cleanse and clear the stones with incense, sage smoke or your breath before reusing them.

Healing

Using a crystal grid for healing is very similar to the way you'd use it for manifesting except that in this case you will be naming the person, describing the healing to take place and, if available, using an image of the person needing to be healed. Of course, you must have the permission of the person who needs healing. Then to set up your grid, place your crystals on the diagram pointed inward, with the central crystal on top of the name, image and description. Consult the crystal list at the back of this book for healing stones that would work best for the situation and add them to your diagram. Then imagine healing light flowing from the outer crystals through the center crystal into the person requiring healing. Take a few moments once a day to focus the healing energy even more strongly through the crystals and stones of the grid. When the person is well, dismantle the grid and cleanse the stones.

Corner-to-Corner Grids

Another crystal grid that is effective and easy to do is the corner-to-corner grid. This is an excellent way to clear and reset the energy of a space as well as to protect it. This grid requires placement of four crystals pointed upward, one for each corner, in the furthermost corners of a room, building or property. If it is possible to set these crystals in a rectangle or square, then that is even better. Once the crystals are placed, stand as close to the center of the area as you can and activate the grid by imagining a big bubble of light spinning in every direction, forwards, backwards, sideways, every way, completely encompassing the four points.

If you want to create a specific type of protective energy or bring a certain energy into the space, select and place stones appropriate to your purpose into a small bag and then suspend them from the ceiling of the center of the area if you are inside, or bury them in the center of the property if outside.

Some years ago I helped a friend do this to increase trade at her resale shop. We placed four citrines (for financial success) in the corners of the store and then hung a small pouch containing stones for luck, money and success in the center of the store. When we activated her crystal grid we put forward the intent that the energy of the stones in the pouch would be incorporated into the energy of the crystal grid. The energy of her store shifted and her clientele increased along with her income. A year later she sold the business for a tidy sum, which she used to purchase a home.

You can also use the corner-to-corner grid to protect or sell your vehicle. Simply tape two crystals, one on each side of the interior of your trunk and two under the hood. If you use duct tape they will likely stay put for a very long time. If you eventually lose a stone you can replace it. This type of grid is useful for protecting you and your family while you are driving. It's worth noting that quartz crystals are ideal because they can be programmed for any purpose, however if you simply want to keep your car running smoothly you could use citrines, or if you want protection from accidents, use amethyst.

Grids on the Go

While it may not be practical to take along many tools for manifesting and healing when on holiday or traveling, it is possible to carry some of the most basic ingredients with you. For example, make or buy a small bag, and place inside it eight small quartz crystals and a slightly larger one along with a green stone, a yellow stone, a red stone and a blue stone. You can even create a small bag with a crystal gridding diagram on it using the instructions for the magical travel altar bag. Carrying such a bag of crystals and stones with you when you travel will ensure you always have the means to create an instant grid anywhere you happen to be.

CHAPTER 11

Goddess Doll

WHEN I WAS two years old my great grandmother gave me my very first doll. She was the size of a real baby and my Memo had made her a little coverall and bonnet that was brown with tiny rosebuds sprinkled all over. She also made her a lovely red corduroy jacket with buttons that looked like tiny red baskets full of colorful flowers. My baby and I went everywhere together. I changed her, fed her, burped her, scolded her and loved her. I trimmed her hair and drew eyebrows on her face with an ink pen and loved and scolded her some more. I still have my doll and I never look at her without fondly recalling our time spent together.

There was Barbie, of course, who I dressed in hand sewn clothes and who drove a pretend car to visit all of her Barbie friends at my other girlfriends' houses. I also made dolls myself, out of old socks, bits of fabric and yarn. As I grew up my interest in dolls did not wane. I began to collect antique dolls and I also continued to make them.

One day it occurred to me that I could make a doll that I could use for more than decoration; one into which I could put my hopes and dreams and my most secret wishes, who could then become a tool through which I could focus my intention for all those wonderful things to become real. This was my very first goddess doll. I named her Bountiful Belle because she was intended to help me bring in more money so that I could live more abundantly. Bountiful Belle did her job very well and I still bring her out when I need a reminder that abundance is only a thought away. Who would have thought that a doll could be the center point of so much power?

Throughout history dolls have been used in one form or another in religious activities, magic rituals and children's play. Dolls were quite common in ancient cultures like China, Babylonia and Egypt across to Greece and Rome. Many of the earliest dolls have been found in graves, indicating that they were cherished enough to be carried with their owners to the next world.

In Egypt, pottery dolls and flat painted wood paddle dolls decorated with strung bead hair have been found in graves and tombs dating as far back as 2000 B.C. Dolls have also been found in the graves of young Roman and Greek children. Interestingly, the graves of older youth do not tend to have dolls present, but it was not because they outgrew them, rather it is believed that the practice was to dedicate their dolls to the goddesses when they reached puberty.

Early dolls were made of basic components such as wood, rags, bone, clay, or sometimes ivory or wax. Primitive dolls were often mere indications of human form though every effort was made to make them as realistic as possible with the limited tools available at the time. By 600 B.C. many dolls were being made with moveable limbs so that they could be bent and posed like real people.

Dolls have been used in ritual practices for centuries, mostly by women but also by men. The magical use of the doll generally has to do with creating an image to represent a person or deity. Goddess dolls were created primarily for magical purposes, to honor the energy of the Goddess and to serve as a repository for that energy. They represent fertility and manifestation, creativity and growth of new things. Goddess dolls that were made to represent a person were often used as focal points for directing attention towards personal goals and intentions. Dolls may also be used as receptacles for prayers.

The energy built up through the process of creating a goddess doll by hand makes it a powerful personal tool. This is not to say that a purchased doll will not be a powerful tool. But just like a wand or other tool you haven't created yourself, you would need to clear and cleanse it of the energy of its creator or previous users before dedicating it for your own personal use.

Making a goddess doll is relatively easy. If you can cut out a small pattern and do a basic running stitch or whip stitch, you can make a doll and personalize it with fabric, beads and other decorations to make it your very own. Goddess dolls can be made for specific purposes, such as representing prosperity, fertility and becoming pregnant. They can be created for year round use and decorated according to the season, or they may be created to represent the energy of a specific goddess or personal goal.

Also, your doll doesn't have to be just like the pattern presented here. There are many variations that you can consider. All you require is some scrap paper to cut out shapes until you have one that you really feel is in tune with what you want to create.

If you want to create a male doll, simply narrow and elongate the body and hips to achieve a more masculine look. You can use a male doll to represent a specific male deity, a manifestation or a desire, or you can decorate it according to the season, just like you can with goddess dolls.

Making Your Own Goddess Doll

You will need:

- Two squares of felt (or 1/4 yd. [22 cm approx.] of fabric in the color you want your doll to be)
- Thread to match the felt/fabric, needle/sewing machine, pins, scissors
- Fabric glue
- Fabric packet containing herbs, crystals, and slips of paper on which to print or write your wishes hopes and dreams
- Colorful fabric scraps, unusual yarns, beads, buttons and other adornments

1. Cut out a paper pattern for your doll. Put two layers of felt/fabric together, right sides facing. Pin your cut paper pattern to the fabric.

2. Trace around the pattern shape on the fabric with chalk or pencil, remove the paper pattern and cut out the pieces.

3. Pin the two pieces together with the right sides facing each other.

4. Using a sewing machine, zig zag or straight stitch around the edge of the fabric, leaving an opening in the lower part of the doll for stuffing. Then turn the doll right side out. If you are hand stitching, whip stitch or straight stitch around the edge of the fabric, leaving an opening.

5. Turn the doll right side out.

6. Begin stuffing your doll with a polyester stuffing such as poly-fill, making sure to pack the filling in fairly tightly, but not so tight that you begin to pull the stitching along the edges. If you prefer to fill your doll with something natural – like buckwheat or rice – keep in mind if the doll should get wet it may mildew or rot with organic material as stuffing.

7. Make a packet. Choose herbs and/or small crystals and stones for the specific purpose you intend for your doll (consult the lists of stone and herb meanings at the back of this book). Then take small slips of paper and write or print on them all the wonderful things you wish to bring into your life. Place these together with the herbs and crystals inside a small square of fabric and use heavy thread or thin ribbon to tie them into a miniature bundle. Place the packet in the center of the stuffing material inside the doll.

8. Once your doll is stuffed, use needle and thread to whip stitch the opening closed. You are now ready to use the embellishments and fabric scraps you gathered to complete your goddess doll.

9. If you want to add facial features to your doll, you can use buttons, beads or embroidery techniques. When planning the location for eyes and mouth it is important to remember that the eyes should be centered in the middle of the head shape and about an eye width apart. The mouth would be about two thirds of the way between the eyes and the imaginary line of the chin. If you put these features too high up in the face area your doll will not look natural.

10. Lengths of yarn or beads may be stitched to the top of the head to make hair. A needle and thread applied to fabric scraps can be used to fashion simple clothing for your doll. You can embellish your decoration with beads and buttons.

Once your goddess doll is complete, cleanse and clear it using your breath, sage or incense smoke, and then sit with it and imagine how you will be using it.

If you are using your doll throughout the seasons you can make sets of clothing that represent the seasons and change its clothes accordingly. If you are using it to help achieve a long term goal you can keep it in a place where you can see and touch it regularly. Other people may think it is just a whimsical doll, and only you will know the powerful intention tool that you have created. If you are using your doll as a prayer doll, you should consider keeping it in a private place where you can pray with it undisturbed.

My Bountiful Prayer

Within this sacred vessel I place my intention for

_____.

May the light of the Universal Source shine
Down upon my creation and bring what
I have called to be into the realm of reality.
Let all five elements,
Earth, Air, Fire, Water and Spirit
Come together to heed my command.
May I look upon this vessel of intention each day
And be grateful for all that I have right now
And all that I have called to me
Through my intention.
And so it is
And so it is
And so it is
It is done.

Goddess Doll Prayer

Beloved Mother Goddess
You hold the mysteries of the darkness
And the bright revelations of the light.
All is born of your fruitful womb.
Your abundance and blessings flow
Freely and with great love for all creatures.
You bring balance and harmony to all creation
And fill each of us with your infinite love.
May I go forth this day with a peaceful heart
And a joyful spirit, knowing that I am always
Protected and provided for.
And so it is.

CHAPTER 12

Promise Plant

OUR CONNECTION to plants goes back as far in history as we do. Plants offered primitive man food between hunts as well as providing herbs for healing remedies and spiritual/magical practices. As man settled into agricultural life and the need to go hunting far and wide diminished, they began to cultivate their own plants and herbs.

Village shamans and healers cultivated plants for magical purposes as well as for healing. They planted their seeds according to the movement of the stars and watered different species of plants with water blessed under specific phases of the moon. As they watered and pruned their plants they spent time blessing and speaking to them about the work they were intended for. By the time they were finally harvested they were supercharged with health and vitality and potency.

For many of us, finding the time to plant and tend a garden properly has become merely a wishful dream. Whereas we once lived in individual dwellings, many now live in duplexes, apartment buildings and high-rise condos. Hence, creating a magical garden has to be approached in a new way. For some, this means using potted plants on a small porch or balcony, for others, a windowsill or kitchen counter. Regardless of how little space we have, however, we can still give our plants the sufficient attention to provide the same positive results.

By creating our own "promise plants" a number of goals may be set to grow together. Plus, it is good feng shui to have healthy living things growing in your home. You can grow a promise plant and imbue it with your intention for any purpose. The more attention you give it, the more you expand the energy of your creation. So it is important to choose a plant you love and a pot that is really pleasing to your eye.

Making Your Own Promise Plant

You will need:

- A large container of clean water drawn at the specific phase of the moon for your purpose. (See the moon phase guide at the back of the book.)
- A small decorative pot that you really like
- 1 large tumbled or rough stone that you can write on with a paint pen
- 8 tiny crystal points (these don't have to be fancy or expensive)
- Paint pen
- Seeds or a seedling (Choose ones that can survive in the light, temperature and moisture environment you can offer.)
- Potting soil

1. Fill your container with water during the phase of the moon appropriate for your purpose then sit with it for a few moments and imagine your love and blessings flowing into it.

2. On the inside of your chosen plant pot, write or draw symbols or images symbolizing whatever it is you wish to manifest. For example, if you will be growing a prosperity promise plant you might draw runes and planetary symbols that have to do with prosperity and financial success. You might even use a green marker pen to take advantage of the color green. Allow paint pen and markers to dry well before proceeding.

3. Take your stone and draw an image or symbol representing your intention. If you wish you may even write your name in celestial script on the other side or draw your zodiac symbol (see appropriate guides at the back of the book). Place the stone over the hole in the pot and lay the small crystal points around it in a circle with the points facing toward the center.

4. If you are planting seeds, fill the pot with soil and make a small hole in the soil to the prescribed depth for that particular seed. Place the seed into the hole and cover it over. If you are transplanting a seedling, add a few inches of soil to the bottom of the pot and place the seedling into the pot so that the top of the root ball is about 1" (25 mm) below the top edge of the pot. Carefully fill in soil around the sides and top and press down gently. Add more to fill if necessary.

5. As soon as you have completed your initial planting, gently water the plant/seed with your blessed water. Keep any leftover water aside for future use. Make sure each month, at the same phase of the moon you draw more water to be used specifically for this plant.

Sit with your pot regularly, visualizing everything you wish to grow in your life, i.e. money, more happiness, a better job, etc. Imagine your intentions coming to fruition as your plant grows and flowers. Put your pot in the location where you will be able to view it often. Water it and take good care of the plant as it begins to grow. Talk to it in a positive way and send it blessings whenever you

are near. Keep it healthy, pruning away dead leaves and spent flowers, picking off marauding invaders, and adding small amounts of organic fertilizer to the soil as needed. Soon you will be enjoying the fruits of your efforts as you experience the vibrant energy of your plant or plants and the positive interaction you have with them. Every time you spend time with your mini-gardening activities you will be reminded that you are bringing your intentions into reality.

You may find promise plants so pleasant to have around that you end up with a small garden of potted promise plants. This is a wonderful way to enjoy the magical energy of plants while you draw positive and wonderful things into your life. And as they grow to maturity, especially if you have chosen to grow some herbs, you can harvest them for your personal use in teas, remedies and magical activities.

CHAPTER 13

Sacred Feather Wand

ONE DAY about five years ago, I was walking on the beach near my home thinking about all of the things I wanted to do and create and wondering how I would ever find the time and wherewithal to do them. At just that moment I looked down and spied a beautiful Scarlet Macaw feather at my feet with its tip barely brushed by an incoming wave. It was a full foot in length and beautifully colored, and I took its presence as a sign to me that my creativity was acknowledged and that my plans would come to fruition in some form or fashion. Since that time I have found feathers now and again, often when I am seeking answers within. Some, like hawk feathers and owl feathers, had to be left where they lay, as some birds are protected and collecting their feathers is illegal. But even so their messages to me were very powerful.

My experience with feathers is not uncommon. I have heard similar stories from people who say they have been "gifted" with feathers. Many of them see feathers as signs, messages or synchronistic events. Feathers put us in mind of freedom, flight and the ability to move above or beyond any boundaries in life. Historically, feathers have been associated with rank, royalty and the spiritual aspects of life. Feathers are used by some cultures as symbols of sacred power. They were also used to indicate status as a shaman, chief, priest or king. For many, feathers are symbolic of the soul itself.

In Ancient Egyptian mythology souls were weighed against a feather after death. The Egyptians believed that the god Anubis would put the soul of the person on one side of a giant scale and then place a feather on the other side. The more bad things one had done in life, the heavier one's soul would be. If it was heavier than a feather the soul was tossed to the monster Am-mit to be devoured, and if it was lighter than a feather the soul was allowed to continue on its path to the heavens.

The Greek myth of Daedalus and Icarus tells the story of how a father and son who were imprisoned in the middle of a labyrinth worked feathers and wax together to make wings so they could escape. The myth goes on to describe how they flew away on their wax and feather wings and how Daedalus had reminded his son Icarus to avoid flying too high. Icarus ignored his father's warning and flew too close to the sun. The wax melted and Icarus fell to the earth and was killed. My grandmother used to tell me the story of Daedalus and Icarus whenever she thought I needed to be reminded to obey my elders.

In the British Isles the Celtic Druids employed feathers in their rituals and ceremonies. The druid priests would wear elaborate robes made of hundreds of feathers in order to invoke the sky gods and gain knowledge of the heavens. Feathers were even used as symbols in the Christian religion to represent the three virtues of faith, hope and charity.

The use of feathers by Native Americans is probably the most well known around the world. Nearly everyone has heard at least one story of the Wild West and Indian warriors sporting single feathers in their head bands and chiefs wearing full head dresses of eagle feathers. Many Native Americans use feathers and feather fans for smudging (where sage smoke is fanned to clear negative energy), in traditional ceremonies and for prayers and healing. In many tribes Eagle feathers are used to carry prayers to the Grandmothers and Grandfathers.

People outside of Native American tribal cultures have also adopted the use of feathers. Alternative healing practitioners use feathers to open chakras and brush down auras. Others use feathers to cleanse their environments through smudging or they keep found feathers as spiritual reminders.

You can use a feather wand to smudge your home or cleanse your aura. Maybe you might use your feather wand to represent the element of air in your personal space. Your own feather wand would make a great addition to your personal spiritual practices and healing activities.

Smudge feathers and feather fans are often made of single wing feathers or a small grouping of feathers. However, in the United States, it is important that you remember that it is illegal to possess the feathers of many raptors (birds of prey). So Owl, Raven, Crow, Hawk. Blue Jay and Eagle feathers, as well as those of some endangered and migratory birds are a big no-no. Fortunately, you can purchase Turkey feathers that have been painted or dyed to look like raptor feathers, if that is what you want to use. Your safest bet is to get your feathers from craft supply stores and specialty shops. That way it is less likely that you will inadvertently end up with an illegal feather in your fan.

Making Your Own Feather Wand

You will need:

- One or more feathers (if using several it is best to choose several sizes)
- A strip of leather or preferred fabric
- E-6000 or Household Goop adhesive
- Superglue
- Scotch tape
- Scissors
- Floss or sinew
- Selection of beads

1. If using leather, cut two pieces, one strip about 1/8" to 1/4" (3 to 6 mm) wide and about 4" (100 mm) long and one about 1" to 2" (25 to 50 mm) wide and 2" (50 mm) long. If you are using fabric, cut one strip about 1" wide and 4" long and twist it to make it a bit more like rope or string. The other piece of fabric should be about 2" wide and 8" to 10" long.

2. If you are using several feathers, use adhesive to glue the tips together to make a small fan. You can even glue them to a small stick, dowel or long crystal, using tape to hold them in place. Allow to dry thoroughly.

3. Take the longer strip, fold it over double and glue it to the bottom 1" (25 mm) of the feather shaft so that the shaft is sandwiched between the two pieces. You may have to hold this in place with a bit of tape until the glue sets well. Once the pieces are firmly attached you may proceed to step 4.

4. Encasing the feather shaft:

   A. For leather, apply a thin coat of glue to the entire inside of the leather piece. Then lay the feather shaft that holds the loop on top of it, situating it so that the loop sticks out about 1/2" (12,5 mm) from the bottom of the leather. Attach one side of the glue-coated leather to the side of the feather shaft or stick. Then gently but firmly begin to roll and wrap the leather piece around the stick/feather shaft until you have rolled it all completely. Make sure you have enough glue on the outer edge to stick it down tightly. Roll the leather onto itself around the feather shaft. Clean off any excess glue, tape down if necessary and allow the area to dry.

B. For fabric, run a thin bead of glue down one edge of the feather and lay the tail end of the fabric on it, situating it so that 1/2" to 3/4" (12,5 to 19 mm) of the loop sticks out from the bottom. Using the same technique described for leather begin to roll the fabric around the feather. Once you feel you have enough rolled to pick it up and manipulate it in your hands, pick it up and pull a little on the fabric while you wind the rest of the fabric around the feather shaft. This will pull the edges down a bit more and gift it a cleaner look. When you get to the last 1/2" of fabric run a light bead of glue along the side of the roll you have created, making sure that it is underneath the area that the last 1/2" will cover. Lay the last bit of fabric over the glue and press it thoroughly until it adheres. If you need to, use tape to hold it in place

5. Once the leather or fabric is dry you can string a long strand of beads to wrap around the shaft. When you have the amount that pleases you, wrap them around to see how far they go. Make sure that they will meet again in the middle with little or no cord or sinew showing. Then spread a thin band of glue in that area of the shaft to hold them in place, rewrap them and tie the ends together. If you have extra, you may wish to add beads to

the hanging strands, tying knots at the ends of the strands to hold them in place. If not, then put a drop of glue on the knot, allow to dry thoroughly and cut away excess.

When your feather fan is finished you should hold a small smudging ceremony with it to cleanse it and set its purpose. If you don't like sage you can use your favorite incense for this purpose.

House Smudging and Blessing

You will need:

- Your new feather wand
- A small shallow bowl or large shell with a little sand in the bottom
- A stick of sage, sweet grass, cedar, or incense of your choice
- Matches or lighter

Use the matches or lighter to light the tip of the smudge stick or incense. With a smudge stick it can take a moment to get it to stay lit and glowing after the flames die out. You might have to blow on it to get it burning well and generating a good amount of smoke. Hold the bowl or shell with your lower three fingers and the smudge stick with your thumb and forefinger, so that the smoking end is suspended over the bowl/shell and sand.

Gently fan the smoke to the North, East, South and West, calling for blessings for your home. Ask that your home be cleansed of negative energy and filled with peaceful and harmonious vibrations. Then begin to walk around your house using the feather wand to waft the smoke in the direction you are moving. Walk around the perimeter of your home's interior making sure to sweep smoke into every corner.

You may even make up your own little prayer or chant that you repeat over and over as you brush the smoke with the fan. When you have completed the rounds of the interior of your home, tip the end of the smudge stick or incense into the sand so that the embers will expire. If you feel uncomfortable about putting out the embers you can leave the stick or incense in the bowl/shell in a safe place where you can keep watch over them while they naturally burn out. Either way, make sure that the smudge stick or incense is cold and free of embers before you store it.

CHAPTER 14

Gemstone Elixirs

CRYSTALS AND MINERALS have been used medicinally for centuries. In fact, some believe that the legendary Atlanteans possessed very advanced techniques that included the use of crystals and minerals in physical healing and rejuvenation.

The ancient Babylonians, as well as the Greeks, Indians, Chinese, and Native Americans used crystals and minerals to heal themselves and their animals. In some of these cultures, expensive and valuable elixirs, ointments and creams were placed in vessels made from precious and semi-precious gemstones to enhance their effectiveness. The Egyptians were known to use elixirs made from gemstones and creams and ointments made from crushed crystals and minerals. Even today crushed minerals are an important component in some medicines as well as in makeup.

Historically, crystals and gemstones have also been laid out on the body to transfer subtle healing energy or incorporated into jewelry for their physical, emotional and spiritual benefits.

How Gemstone Elixirs Work

Today, crystals and minerals are included in homeopathic remedies (diluted and potentized substances used internationally for healing). In fact, as more scientific evidence emerges to support the existence of subtle energy, uncut crystals, rough and polished minerals and cut gemstones are enjoying a resurgence of popularity in diverse healing practices.

Crystals and semi-precious stones (especially crystals) have the ability to store, transform and transmit a variety of energies. This means that they can absorb any negative energies that might be responsible for imbalance or disease in the body, as well as transmit balancing and healing energies into the body to restore health to it.

Each crystal or mineral has the ability to transmit a specific wavelength to the body, as well as a specific effect that can be used for healing. Combinations of minerals and crystals also can be used to address different aspects or symptoms of an illness, disease or imbalance on the physical, mental, emotional and spiritual levels.

Gemstone elixirs are tinctures that are produced by exposing distilled water to the vibrational energies of specific crystals or minerals. Sometimes these are prepared by immersing the crystal or mineral in the distilled water for a prescribed period; other times they are prepared by simply placing the distilled water near the crystals. As one consumes the elixir, usually by taking small doses over a period of time, the vibrational essences work on the root cause of "disease" within the mental, physical, emotional or spiritual body, thereby enabling the individual to clear the issues that created the dis-ease. Elixirs are very simple to create. They can be made fresh for immediate consumption or they can be preserved and used sublingually over a period of time.

The most important part of a gemstone elixir is the stone or crystal from which the essence is created. You may choose crystals and stones according to their healing properties, or you can use your intuition and pick stones according to how and what you feel when you hold them.

If you are unsure which stones to choose you can use kinesiology testing (muscle strength testing) to help you make choices. This is easy. You stretch out your left arm and make it stiff and strong. Have someone test its strength by pressing gently down at the wrist. Then, hold the stone in your right hand and have the same person press down on your left outstretched arm with the same pressure at the wrist to see how "strong" you are with the stone. If your arm is hard to press down (indicating strength), the stone will be good for you to use.

If it is easy to press down (indicating weakness) then this is a sign that the stone is not the right choice for you at this time. If you get an unclear answer (the arm goes down a bit, but the indication is not really clear) you can rebalance your system by tapping on a point in the middle of your chest in line with the nipples 20 to 30 times, and then tap again 20-30 times on a point about 1-1/2" (25-12,5 mm) below your navel, before repeating the question. You should get a much clearer answer.

If you are alone you can "sway" test by holding the stone to your heart and making the statement, "This _____ (state the name of the mineral or crystal) is good for me to use for _____ (state the purpose for which you wish to use it)." Then stand still and notice whether your body starts swaying in a forward or backward motion. Forward usually indicates yes and backward is usually no. If you do not find yourself swaying in either direction then there is no yes or no answer at this time.

Making Elixirs with Single or Multiple Stones

You can make an elixir with one crystal, create a set of single crystal elixirs to mix as needed, or you can create elixirs with a grouping of stones for a specific purpose. Elixirs are relatively inexpensive to make and easy to store or replace. Several drops under the tongue or in water several times a day are commonly used for desired results.

Sometimes mixing crystal vibrations in one elixir is easier than making a lot of separate ones and then taking a number of them for the desired result. If you are in a big hurry, it is nice to be able to grab the single elixir bottles you need and mix drops of them into another bottle to create a combination elixir.

The most important thing about making elixirs from crystals and stones is to make sure that the stones you use are not water-soluble and do not contain mercury, arsenic, copper, or other toxic substances. One way to determine if the stone you are about to use is not suitable for traditional elixir preparation is to look in a really good mineral guide to find out what the stone's physical properties are.

You might be surprised to find that some stones, like malachite for example, cannot be used in water to prepare an elixir. Generally, stones from the quartz family, such as clear or smoky quartz, amethyst, citrine, rose quartz or aventurine, are considered to be safe to use as long as they do not have other minerals included in their matrix. When in doubt, use the method here that does not involve putting crystals or stones directly in contact with water.

Making Your Own Gemstone Elixirs

You will need:

- Pure distilled water
- Clean clear glass or crystal containers that will allow light to pass through
- White or light cheesecloth like fabric
- Rubber bands
- Crystals and stones
- If you are going to make an elixir to drink right away these items may be all you will need. If you are going to store and use the elixirs over a period of time you will also require:
- Medium sized dark bottles
- Small dosage bottles with droppers (pipettes)
- Preservative (such as vegetable glycerin, brandy or apple cider vinegar)

Before you begin make sure that all of your containers and bottles and stones are carefully washed, thoroughly rinsed and have been air-dried.

1. Place your container on a tray or board (such as a cutting board).

2. Put the chosen stones in a clear glass jar or container filled with distilled water. If you are using stones that should not be in water, place them around the outside edge of the container so that they are touching the glass.

3. Cover the top of the container with some light cheesecloth or cotton to pre-vent contamination by leaves and bugs or other organic matter. You can use a rubber band to secure the fabric cover to the container.

4. Place your quartz crystals in a circle around the container with the points turned in towards the center.

5. Set the container out in full bright sunlight for at least an hour. Caution! If you leave a container in the sunshine with any clear crystals surrounding it, be sure to put it on a table or stay close by. Quartz can magnify the sun's energy and start a FIRE if you leave it in the grass.

6. To preserve an elixir, pour a small amount (5-10 drops) of brandy, vegetable glycerin or apple cider vinegar into the water. This will stabilize the vibra-tional energies and preserve the mixture. Once you have preserved your elixir you can pour it into a dark bottle. This first preparation is called the "mother bottle" or mother tincture.

7. To prepare either a combination or single dosage bottle, pour distilled wa-ter into a small one-ounce bottle until it is three-quarters full. Then fill to the top with your preservative and add several drops of elixir from your mother tincture. Once you have prepared your dosage bottle you will want

to shake it hard for several minutes or pound the bottom of it on your palm (but not so hard you break the bottle). This is similar to the process of percussion that homeopaths use to set the energies of substances in homeopathic remedies. In fact, it is a good idea to shake or "percuss" your dosage bottle every time you prepare to take an elixir. You may then use several drops under the tongue or drink a glass of pure water, with several drops of your dosage elixir added, at least four times daily.

8. It's important to be diligent about marking your prepared elixirs, mother tinctures and dosage bottles very carefully. Each bottle should be labeled with:

A. The stones and preparation technique used.
B. The date the elixir was started.
C. Whether the bottle is a mother bottle or dosage bottle.

If you do this you will avoid having a cabinet full of elixirs that you can't really use because you don't know for sure what is in them.

You can supercharge any elixir during the preparation stage by leaving it to sit in the light of either the sun or the moon during the time of the full moon or new moon. You can charge it up even more by placing it in a dark spot, after energizing it in the sun, and surrounding the container with quartz points all pointing towards the container. You can leave this for a week or so while it receives added amplification from the quartz points. Afterwards you may preserve the elixir and create your mother tincture and dosage bottles.

Elixirs may be used in alignment with the lunar calendar. This can be done with elixirs created for both people and pets. Some people feel that starting with new moon or full moon energy adds to an elixir's potency. It is also a good way of keeping track of the time you are taking them (from one moon to the next), as most elixirs are only needed for a month or so.

If you have been taking an elixir and are unsure if you still need to continue, you can use the body sway technique to find out if it is still necessary. All you do is hold the elixir and state "I still need to take this _____ (insert the name of your elixir)." A body sway backward will let you know that it is time to stop.

Other Uses for Gemstone Elixirs

Elixir Sprays

Elixir sprays are easy to make by adding several drops of elixir to distilled water. Elixir sprays are perfect for space clearing in situations when incense or sage cannot be used.

Elixir Baths

You can enjoy a gemstone elixir bath by dropping a teaspoon or so of elixir into your bath water. It is like taking the stones in the bath with you, without the risk to the stones or to the body (sitting on a sharp crystal can be very painful!).

Pet Elixirs

Elixirs can be safely used for pets IF you are absolutely sure of the safety of the stones you prepared them with, or if they are prepared with the alternative technique of leaving the stones outside the container. The simplest way to give pets an elixir is to put a few drops into their water every day until the problem dissipates. Be sure to contact your vet for serious problems.

It is important to understand that elixirs are not intended to take the place of traditional medical care. When in doubt, always consult your health professional.

CHAPTER 15

Protection Pentagram

WHEN I WAS younger I remember watching scary movies that showed people drawing pentagrams on rough attic floorboards and placing black candles at the points so they could control or harm someone in some terrifying way. The images in the movies really did frighten me, but as I got older it occurred to me that the same five-pointed star shape portrayed in those movies also could be found in non-threatening forms all around me.

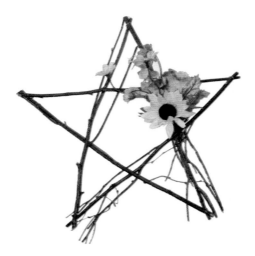

For instance, I was born in Texas, which is known as "The Lone Star State." It has a single five-pointed star on the state flag. The U.S. flag displays fifty white pentagrams floating on a field of blue. Christmas trees around the globe are topped with shining stars every year. The pentagram was one of the very first complex geometric shapes I learned how to draw at school and I loved filling pages with them. There is something complete and solid about a pentagram that I find grounding and comfortable, so it is not surprising to me that, in spite of Hollywood, the pentagram has become a much more widely used and accepted symbol today.

The pentagram has an ancient and honorable history and has held great significance for many cultures and religions. The first recorded pentagram may be from ancient Mesopotamia where it was found on pot shards that date back as far as 3500 B.C. It is believed that the pentagram was somehow tied in with early written forms of language.

Since that time the pentagram has worn many hats, so to speak. For the ancient Hebrews the pentagram represented the five books of the Torah and was a valued and sacred symbol. After studying the origin and use of the pentagram, Pythagoras declared it to be geometrically sound, calling it an "emblem of true perfection." Later the Druids adopted the pentagram as a symbol of the God-head. Celtic pagans also were attracted to the pentagram and came to use it to symbolize the goddess Morrigan.

Some may be surprised to know that Early Christians also used the pentagram. Before the symbol of the cross was introduced, the pentagram was honored as a representation of the five wounds of Christ. Though the cross was adopted as the official symbol of Christ sometime during the 4th century A.D., the pentagram continued to be used as a Christian symbol. By the medieval period many people were using the pentagram to protect against demons.

The Knights Templar, Christian monk soldiers from the time of the Crusades, adopted the pentagram into their mystic symbolism. And the mystic value of the pentagram was not lost on early pagans who incorporated it into their customs and worship to represent the five elements: earth, air, fire, water and spirit. For many centuries the pentagram had a very positive connotation.

It wasn't until the Inquisition in Europe that pentagrams were given a negative meaning. Christian Inquisitors, who had at one time ignored natural paganism, took notice when pagan practitioners tried to assassinate them in an attempt to stop the torture and murder perpetuated by the Inquisition. This led to an all out effort to stamp out all forms of natural or pagan worship, and it was for this reason that the Inquisitors declared the traditional pagan symbol of the pentagram to be the symbol of Satan. For many years afterwards pentagrams were classed with the worst of evils and even possessing one could lead to execution.

In recent times the pentagram became re-popularized as a positive symbol, used in protective amulets and adopted by many Wiccans as a symbol of Spirit and the Elements. Many people now view pentagrams as symbolic of earth awareness and the desire to honor the planet and become better stewards of it. While Christian groups in general may still feel somewhat uncomfortable with the pentagram, it has lost much of the stigma it has carried since the days of the Inquisition. The reputation of the pentagram appears to have come full circle to be restored to acceptability in current culture.

The Locations and Meanings of the Points of the Pentagram

Earth:	Lower left hand point	Stability and Physical Endurance
Fire:	Lower right hand point	Courage and Daring
Water:	Upper right hand point	Emotions and Intuition.
Air:	Upper left hand point	Intelligence and the Arts
Spirit:	Top	Divinity, God, All that Is, Deity

Making Your Own Protective Pentagram

Making your own protective pentagram is a wonderful way to bring very positive energy into your home while keeping negative energy out. It can be made of nearly any kind of branch such as willow, grape vine, birch, ash, etc. It is best if you can get fresh branches smaller than the width of your pinkie finger and still green, so that they have a bit more flexibility. (See the wood key for the properties of several commonly used woods.)

You will need:

- Green branches (a pinky finger width or less)
- Wire to bind them and create a hanger on the back (Floral wire will work though for thick branches you may need to double it.)
- E6000 or Household Goop adhesive (glue gun and glue sticks if desired)
- Garden shears or small saw
- Wire nips
- Beads, ribbons, crystals and other embellishments
- Scissors
- Tape

1. Cut five branches in equal lengths. Use wire to tightly tie the ends of two sticks together with stick 2 attached over the top of stick 1. Make sure that the twisting of the wire is done from the back side on all of the attachments.

2. Attach stick 3 to the top of the unattached end of stick 2 being sure that the body of stick 3 lies underneath stick 1. Be careful to tighten the wire well.

3. Thread stick 4 over stick 1 and under stick 2. Use your wire to attach the end firmly over the top of the end of stick 3. The weaving you just did should give your project a bit more stability.

4. Thread stick 5 over stick 2 and under stick 3. Attach one end of stick 5 over the end of stick 4 and under the open end of stick 1.

5. Now that you have all of the sticks wired together, turn the piece over to the side with twisted wire ends showing. Clip off the excess wire down to 1/4" (6 mm) from each twist. Gently manipulate your pentagram until you feel that it looks fairly proportional (it won't be perfect because sticks aren't perfectly straight). Once you are satisfied with the shape, tuck the twisted ends of the wires against the sticks on the back side and add a drop of glue to each to protect them and keep them in place. Next, go around the outer edges and add a dab of glue to each junction, and add dabs of glue to the inner junctions created by your weaving. Set aside and allow all of the glue to dry completely before continuing.

6. Now that your base is created, take a loop of wire and attach it to the tip of the point you choose for the top.

7. Your magical protection pentagram can be decorated with any number of items, particularly ones that have specific meanings to you or that have color, crystal or herb qualities you wish to impress it with. Wire, ribbons, beads, crystals, fabrics and found items can all be used to add energy to your protection pentagram, just as you might use such things to add to other magical tools.

Your protection pentagram should be hung on the front door of your home. Before you hang it you should take a few moments to sit with it to imagine what it will be doing for you and your family and then say a short prayer such as this one (or you can make up your own):

I call upon the Five Elements
That each point of the pentagram represents
Earth, Air, Fire, Water, and Spirit
To protect this home and all within
Nourish us and keep us safe from all harm
And so it is.

In addition to using a larger pentagram for your home you can use thinner and smaller twigs to create miniature versions to tuck into a kitchen window or grace a narrow wall. Pentagrams are not only considered protective but lucky as well, in the same way that upturned horseshoes are. Large or small, decorated pentagrams make beautiful hand-crafted gifts for just about any occasion.

CHAPTER 16

Crystal Casting Set

CRYSTAL CASTING is a form of divination whose roots date back to biblical times and beyond. The Urim and Thummin of the ancient Hebrews, described in the Old Testament, were divinatory stones which the high priest consulted regarding matters affecting the welfare of the children of Israel. Sadly the Old Testament doesn't give many clues as to how, specifically, the stones were utilized. The Old Testament also refers to the breastplate or chest piece of the Hebrew high priest, which was embedded with twelve stones, each of which represented one of the twelve tribes of Israel. Apparently, this "garment" was used to divine the will of God. Again, however, we have no details as to how it worked, although we do have a list of the stones used.

No fairy tale or fantasy movie is complete without the appearance of crystal balls or divinatory methods of some kind. Over the ages there have been many methods of reading the auguries and divining the future, from killing goats, sheep (and sometimes even people) in order to study their entrails, to filling golden dishes with water, to breathing gasses seeping up through rocks in order to facilitate trance states, as is alleged to have been the case with the famous Oracle of Delphi. Thankfully, the methods in use today are so much easier, far more humane and a lot more fun. Indeed, I have been using crystals in divination for many years and have tried several methods developed by others. Eventually, however, I developed my own casting plan and technique for reading the stones. This has proved so successful that I was commissioned by Planetlightworker, an international metaphysical magazine published monthly online (*www.planetlightworker.com*) to produce an exclusive column called the Crystal Star Oracle Reading for their newsletter.

Many fabrics lend themselves well to the creation of a casting cloth, but if your sewing skills are an issue you can simply purchase a non-patterned scarf.

While it may take a bit more effort to acquire the stones for a crystal casting set, it's well worth investing the time and effort in searching them out as this will really add to their energy and power. Crystal and metaphysical shops are good places to look for medium and small tumbled stones (3/4" to 1" stones are best). You can also search for tumbled stones online if you are having difficulty finding some of the ones you need.

Making a Crystal Casting Set

You will need:

- An 18"-20" (45-50 cm) square of solid color fabric or a solid color scarf
- A large sheet of paper to draw your design on
- Sewing transfer paper
- Paint pen or fabric dye pens (gold and silver are best on dark fabrics)
- Pencil
- Ruler
- Protractor or assortment of circular shapes to trace around
- 12 -24 or more tumbled stones that feel right to you (there is a stone list in the back of this book that may help)

1. Plan your design for the diagram to go on the casting cloth and draw it on a piece of paper. There are several examples of casting cloth designs as well as instructions for readings at the end of this chapter. You might even design your very own diagram.

2. Use sewing transfer paper to transfer your design to the appropriate side of the fabric.

3. Use your paint pen or fabric dye pen to lightly draw the diagram on the fabric. Allow to dry.

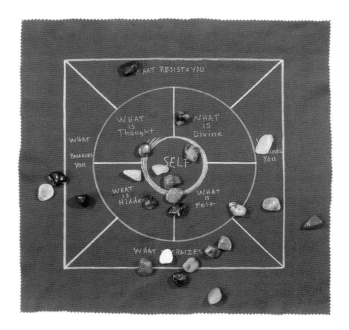

4. Gather tumbled stones for your casting cloth.

5. Consider fashioning a pouch or bag to hold your cloth and stones (you'll find instructions for this in Chapter 20).

Once you have assembled your casting set, cleanse it in incense, sage smoke or your breath, and sit with it imagining how you will be using it. Then try it out. Ask your questions and cast your stones. Casting stones is an art that is developed over time and the more you practice with your crystal casting set the more skilled you will become. You may even develop your own ideas for diagrams that will better suit your needs.

When you make a casting cloth it is a good idea to make a card reminding you of the meaning of each quadrant and the order in which you will read the stones, plus a list of your stones and at least a keyword describing each one. This will help you access the information quickly as you practice, and eventually you will naturally recognize the meanings of the stones in relation to their locations on the casting cloth. The techniques used in reading crystals on a casting cloth may also be done with runes.

Here are some sample Casting Cloth designs and reading techniques:

Five Quadrant Reading

Concentrate on the issue or situation you want enlightenment about. Reach into your bag of stones, draw one out and place it in the center of the diagram, then draw out another and place in the south quadrant. Draw another for the West quadrant, the North quadrant, and finally the East quadrant. Begin your reading in the center, then move to the South quadrant and start working your way around clockwise. This is one of the best and easiest ways to start learning how to cast a reading.

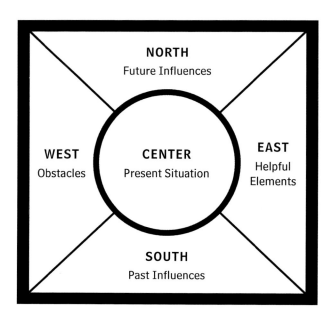

As you get more confident or would like a more in depth reading, simply tip the stones out of the bag onto the diagram and, using the same order described above, read each quadrant in turn. You may find that while some quadrants may have no stones in them others may have several. Don't worry about this. Quadrants with no stones indicate that either information about that specific area of life is unknown at this time or there's no need for any information. Quadrants with many stones, however, indicate that there is much to learn about the question you have posed or the issue you are examining relating to that area.

Nine Quadrant Reading

Pose a question or think about a situation or issue you need more information about. Cast all of the stones upon the cloth. Read the stones in the center ring first (see diagram). Next, read the stones in each quadrant of the second ring, starting with the upper left quadrant and moving clockwise. Finally, read the stones in the South, West, North and East quadrants of the outer ring.

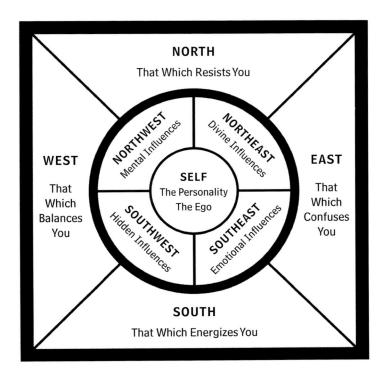

Twelve Houses Reading

Pose a question and toss the crystals on the cloth. Read the stones in each quadrant, starting with the first house and moving through to the twelfth house. You can also do this reading, treating the houses as the months of the year (1 = January, etc.), to see what the coming year may bring, or to look at the next twelve months as they relate to a specific issue or situation.

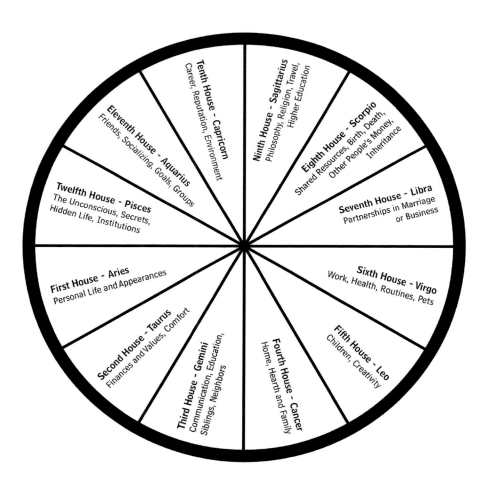

CHAPTER 17

Magic Beeswax Candle

FOR OVER 5000 years candles have been used as a primary light source. Originally, they were made from boiled and rendered animal fat (often referred to as tallow), or seeds and plants that exuded waxy substances.

Long before it became a popular material for candle making, beeswax was prized as an important component in the embalming processes used by the early Persians. Because it was clean, fragrant and malleable enough to shape, the Ancient Egyptians employed it to preserve the paintings inside their tombs, while the Romans used it to fashion death masks as well as life-sized figures.

During the early Middle Ages, as the Church began to gain in wealth, it soon came to recognize the value of candles that did not produce much smoke, and thus did not cause a build-up of grime on their valuable and sometimes priceless works of religious art. The fact that it was also pure and sweet-smelling only added to the desirability of beeswax as a candle making material. Because it was considered to be so pure and clean, beeswax candles came to be associated with the purity of Jesus through his virgin birth of the Holy Mother Mary. The Catholic Church called for the use of only 100% pure beeswax candles in religious ceremonies, and in England strictly-enforced laws protected and promoted the purity of beeswax candles.

At that time bees were wild so beeswax was not easy to come by. Bees make beeswax as a by-product of honey, which they manufacture from the nectar of flowers. It takes eight pounds of honey to make one pound of beeswax. This made beeswax candles very expensive items that only the Church, wealthy nobles and Royalty could afford. Beeswax candle making became so well perfected that by the 9th century 24-hour beeswax candles could be relied upon to help one tell the time of day or night. Beeswax candles remained the most popular and cleanest light source for centuries, until the early 1900s when electricity brought artificial light into many homes.

Beeswax candles are still used in many churches today and are currently enjoying a resurgence of popularity among the general public as well as religious and spiritual groups. Flat 8" x 16" (20 x 40 cm) sheets of honeycomb-pressed beeswax are available in a variety of colors to be made into personalized candles for use in the home and in personal or group ceremonies.

I learned how to make rolled beeswax candles from my friend, Diana DiSimone, who not only taught me how to roll them, but also how to use small crystals, herbs and oils to infuse them with fragrance as well as specific energies aligned to whatever goal I might be using the candles for. She even taught me how to make two-toned candles, which are attractive and further incorporate the use of color energy in candle making. I was surprised and pleased at how easy and fun beeswax candles are to make and use.

You can enjoy the process of making beeswax candles for your home and for your own spiritual or magical purposes. Many colors of wax sheets and proper wick can be obtained from a local metaphysical shop or you can search the Internet to find one of the many online outlets. Many of the herbs, essential oils, crystals and stones you might want to use may be found in the same ways. It's also worth checking out your local bead supply shops for small crystals, in the form of chip beads, which usually come in sixteen-inch strands, and are excellent for embedding lightly into candles. The herbal, crystal, and color key guides at the back of the book will help you choose the best ones for your purpose.

Making a Beeswax Candle

You will need:

- Sheets of beeswax in appropriate colors
- A length of wick at least 1" (25 mm) longer than the width of the wax sheet
- A large piece of cardboard or smooth plastic chopping board to roll on (to protect your table from wax)
- A sharp knife or scissors
- Any small crystals, oils and/or herbs you want to add to the candle
- Colored super fine glitter, if desired, to add sparkle to your candle

1. Lay the beeswax sheet onto the cardboard so that the longest part is facing lengthwise.

2. Lay your cut length of wick on the bottom edge with a bit hanging over at either end. Then fold and press down the edge of the wax sheet over the candle wick. You want to be sure that the wax is pressed against the wick so that it will burn better when lit.

3. Begin to roll the candle. Use a firm hand but don't press too hard as you roll, and make sure that the body of the candle stays straight. If you are using a full sheet, roll the candle about a third of the way and stop.

4. Take any small crystals you plan to use and hold them in your palm while envisioning how they will add their energy to your candle. Then gently press your crystals into the wax near the bottom of the candle and roll the wax just past them.

5. Take any herbs you have chosen and spend a few moments meditating on the energy they will bring to the candle you are making. Sprinkle the herbs sparingly across several inches of the candle sheet and then roll the candle far enough to cover the herbs. If you are heavy handed with your herbs they may catch fire as the candle burns, so err on the side of caution when adding herbs to your candle.

6. Put one or two drops of the fragrant oils you have chosen into your hands and gently inhale their scent as you envision how they will help you to reach whatever goal you will set with the burning of the candle. Rub your hands together and then rub the inside of the flat sheet of candle with the oils while continuing to think about the power you are generating and infusing into your candle. If you are using pure essential oils you may want to simply

allow two or three drops to fall on the remainder of the wax sheet and avoid contact with your skin. Roll the candle until the rest of the wax sheet has been taken up.*

7. Gently press the wax edge into the candle body taking care not to press too hard. Then curl the bottom bit of wick in a circle and press into the wax on the bottom of the candle.

8. Holding the candle in your hand, press the bottom against the flat surface of the cardboard to flatten it.

9. You can press the top down gently to create a flat or tapered edge and then trim the wick so that it sticks up about 1/4" (6 mm).

10. If you want to make your candle sparkle you can dust it with super fine glitter and rub it gently with your hands to help the glitter stick to the candle.

Two-Toned Candles

To make two-toned candles, start with your basic color and roll until there is about 3" (75 mm) left flat. Then lay the second sheet near the body of the candle and continue to roll until all of the wax is used. During the process you can add crystals, herbs and oils as described above.

By carefully folding flat sheets in half and back again, you will eventually get the beeswax sheet to break cleanly along the crease. This will enable you to create different size sheets for different size candles. A full sheet will make a fat 8" (20 cm) tall candle. A half sheet will make a thinner version. To make short fat candles simply fold your sheets lengthwise and divide along the crease.

* Caution

When using essential oils it is very important to be aware of any contraindications relating to specific health conditions. Essential oils are extremely powerful and it is not uncommon for some people to have allergic reactions. For example, epileptics should not use Rosemary oil as it could trigger seizures. More and more people are also becoming allergic to Lavender oil for some unknown reason. Another point to bear in mind with essential oils is that less is more. Too much oil in your candle, for example, could easily transform it into a fire hazard. Plus, while two or three drops of oil can act as a remedy for a specific condition, i.e., 2-3 drops of Lavender oil can be used for banishing headaches, any more than could actually do the reverse and worsen the condition. So do remember to always treat essential oils with great respect and caution.

Beeswax Candle Recipes for Specific Purposes

- House Blessing Candle
- Brown beeswax
- Jasper and/or Tiger Eye chips
- Essential oils/herbs: Angelica, Marjoram, Rose Geranium
- Romance Candle
- Pink and/or Red beeswax
- Rose Quartz chips
- Essential oils/herbs: Rose, Vanilla, Geranium
- Healing Candle
- Blue beeswax
- Malachite chips
- Essential oils/herbs: Sandalwood, Chamomile, Eucalyptus
- Prosperity Candle
- Green and/or Gold beeswax
- Citrine and/or Garnet chip
- Essential oils/herbs: Thyme, Cinnamon, Mint, Basil

CHAPTER 18

Dream Pillow

DREAMING IS SOMETHING that we all do every night while we sleep, even if we don't remember what we dream, or we only remember tiny bits and snatches. Our dreams are symbolic language that our subconscious uses to communicate with us while we sleep. That sounds simple enough, but many people scratch their heads and puzzle over the meanings of their dreams. The images and symbols in dreams are often like secret code – highly personal and important – and can only truly be interpreted by the person having the dream. Some people simply dream and do not feel led to try to understand any aspects of their dreams.

Some want to understand their dreams better or direct their dreams in a certain way. Many people who want to direct their dreams or stop having certain kinds of dreams utilize the power of herbs to assist in the process.

People have always been fascinated with the other world of dreaming and have wished to understand the meaning of their dreams or to control and manipulate their dream state in some way. Current terminology, such as 'lucid dreaming', 'dream journeying' and 'dream interpretation' describe ways in which people continue to try to understand and control their dreams even today.

In the past, combinations of herbs were often used to facilitate dream activities in addition to helping stop nightmares, alleviate headaches and reduce physical pain. The easiest and safest way to use herbs for sleep was to place them into a small pillow that could be slept with.

Pillows date back to the time of ancient Egypt but for many centuries were objects that only royalty and the very rich could afford. Those who could not afford pillows slept with small sachets of herbs placed near their face or hung them around their neck. People who could afford pillows would place the scented sachets near or under their sleeping pillow. As the person rolled during the night the herbs would be jostled and crushed releasing fragrances designed to facilitate or manipulate their dreams in some way or another.

When I began my spiritual exploration I became very interested in what my dreams had to tell me. So I bought books on dream interpretation and kept a journal by the bed to write down any dreams I had before I could forget them. Then one evening I attended a class on how to make and use dream pillows. Making my very own dream pillow was fun, and exploring the herbs and crystals to use to boost my dreaming was fascinating. But what was really interesting was the dream I had the first night I placed my new dream pillow inside my pillowcase.

As I went to bed I took a moment to become calm and centered and then asked for my dreams to tell me what I could do to help restore balance to the planet. That night I dreamed that I was a beautiful goddess about nine or ten feet tall, and I was dressed in the most amazing garment of living green, shimmering with color and light. I could shoot fire out of my index fingers, and I used my right finger to shoot eleven holes in the ground in a large circle around me and then another 22 in an even larger circle. I remember feeling incredibly powerful and strong and very connected to the planet. That dream led me to plant a special grid of crystals in my own back yard, which I used regularly to generate and build energy to give to the Earth. I have to say that every time I worked with my grid I felt I became the "green goddess," commanding and potent and very capable of directing powerful healing energy deep into the Mother Earth.

I don't always have such strong dreams when I sleep with my dream pillow, but I have noticed that I always dream when I use it and I remember more of my dreams and the feelings that are associated with them. I have also become pretty good at remembering and interpreting the very personal symbolic messages my subconscious mind sends to me through my dreams.

You can enjoy the positive effects of an herbal dream pillow by making one for yourself. Dream pillows are very easy to create and can be as simple as a filled muslin bag with the end sewn shut or can be as elaborate as a shaped pillow of fancy fabrics adorned with beads and other embellishments. As you are planning your own dream pillow you may wish to take into account what color and texture of fabric is the most pleasing and relaxing for you to see and touch. And, while most dream pillows are square or rectangular in shape, don't feel you have to be limited by this. You can make them circular, oval or maybe even in the general shape of your favorite animal or totem. You are only limited by your imagination and your sewing ability.

Make Your Own Dream Pillow

- You will need:
- Decorative fabric
- Matching thread
- 4" x 5" (100 x 125 mm) mesh bag to hold herbs
- Snaps or Velcro if desired for the closure
- Needle or sewing machine
- Straight pins
- Ruler
- Scissors
- Chosen herbs
- Beads or other embellishments as desired

1. Fold the fabric with the right sides facing each other. Use the ruler to draw a 5" x 6" (125 x 150 mm) rectangle on the wrong side of the fabric. Pin the layers of fabric together so that they don't slide or move around, and then cut the shape out.

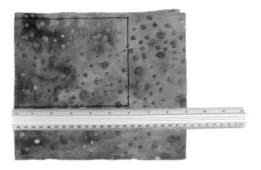

2. Keep the right sides of the fabric pinned together while you hand or machine stitch the edges, leaving a half inch margin all the way around three edges, and leaving one end open.

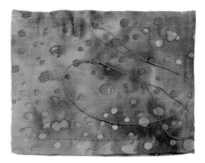

3. Turn the pillow right side out and tuck the ends under by ½" to leave a finished edge. If you wish to add beads or other decorations do so now, keeping in mind that you will want to keep the end of your pillow easily accessible.

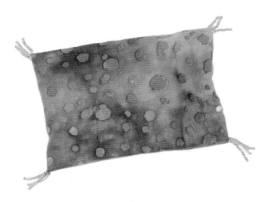

4. Mix the herbs and flowers you wish to use in a bowl. You may wish to add a few drops of essential oil to enhance the power of the herbs. Then fill the bag but avoid overstuffing it. The herbs need to be a bit loose inside so the air can circulate through the bag and release the scents.

5. Tie the bag shut and insert it into the pillow. You can baste the open edge shut or put snaps or a bit of Velcro on it so that it can be easily opened to change out old herbs for fresh ones.

6. Once your pillow is ready to use you may wish to sit with it for a few moments and envision how the pillow will work for you. See yourself enjoying the results of using your dream pillow. Then place it between your sleeping pillow and its cover before you go to sleep.

Choosing the Herbs for Your Dream Pillow

There are a great variety of herbs and flowers you can use to fill your dream pillow, and single herbs or specific combinations of herbs can be chosen for a variety of purposes. You can research and choose herbs yourself or you can use recipes created by others.

Drops of essential oils or small crystals and stones may also be added to your herb mixture to enhance the energy. I learned this from the lady who taught me how to make dream pillows. She would choose her herbs and then add several tiny crystals to the mix. She insisted that it made the pillows more powerful and the essential oils helped the fragrance to last longer. One of my clients tried adding small tumbled lepidolites to the dream pillow she was making to help her sleep more soundly. She reported several weeks later that the lepidolite-laden pillow was working wonderfully and that she hadn't enjoyed such good sleep in years.

Some Herbal Recipes for Dream Pillows to get You Started

For protection:

- 1 part Myrrh
- 1 part Patchouli
- 1 part Rosemary
- 1 part Rose Geranium

For headaches:

- 1 part Bergamot
- 1 part Lavender flowers
- 1 part Mint

(To make it even more aromatic you can add 2-3 drops of pure essential oil of Lavender. However, do be careful not to use more than this amount, as essential oils are extremely powerful, and adding too many drops can actually create the very symptoms you are trying to cure.)

If you want to make a heat or cold pack to use for headaches and migraine, you can add 1 part Eucalyptus to the above mix and stir the whole thing together with 1-2 cups of uncooked rice. This bag can be kept in the freezer as a cool pack or be heated in the microwave for 60 seconds or less.

For pleasant dreams:

- 1 part Rosemary
- 1 part Mugwort
- 2 parts Rose Petals
- 2 large pinches of Mint
- 5 or 6 Cloves

For cleansing and clearing:

- 1 part Cinnamon
- 1 part Cloves
- 1 part Jasmine
- 1 part Sandalwood
- 1 part Lavender

For sweet and peaceful sleep:

- 1 part Rosemary
- 1 part Lavender
- 1 part Sweet Hops
- 1 part Rose Petals

To stop nightmares:

- 1 part Thyme
- 1 part Mugwort
- 2 parts Pennyroyal
- 2 parts Basil
- Several drops of oil of Lavender

Psychic enhancement:

- 1 part Sandalwood
- 1 part Sage
- 1 part Anise
- 1 part Mugwort
- 1 part Nutmeg

A Short Prayer for Your Dream Pillow

I call upon the Divine in dreamtime
to bring me what I seek.
May love shine down from above
to keep me while I sleep.
Sweet pillow gift me with your scent
throughout the long, dark night,
And bring to me what I have wished
At dawn's first golden light.

A note about the use of herbs: Any time you plan to use herbs, even for a pillow stuffing, you should be confident that you are not allergic to any of them. Some people have reactions to some plants. If the herbs in your dream pillow cause you to have allergic responses you should remove them and choose different herbs.

CHAPTER 19

Secret Journal

KEEPING A JOURNAL is one of the best things I have ever done for myself and for my writing. I have used journals to hold my secret thoughts, art sketches, concerns, dreams, poetry, and even my computer passwords. My journals provide me a place to record daily activities and events as well as my thoughts, feelings, ideas and plans. Writing in them helps me to express myself safely and privately, like when I am angry with my boss or feel especially passionate about a situation or issue, without having to act on my feelings.

My old journals have become almost like a personal history that I can refer back to whenever I want to remember something in more detail or find a previously recorded idea or piece of text that I am now ready to use.

Journaling has increased in popularity as people have become more interested in personal exploration and self-expression. Bookstores around the world now have whole sections devoted to personal journals and diaries of every shape and size, lined and unlined, fine paper and handmade paper. Some are hard backed, some soft, and some have special catches or wrappings to keep them closed when not in use.

Of course, you don't have to have a fancy journal to keep personal writings in. Some of my best journaling has been done in spirals or composition books. But there is something extra nice about wrapping an attractive cover around your own personal writings. A beautiful binding on the outside can reinforce the feeling that there is something very special inside.

The use of journals can be traced back to the ancient Chinese around 56 A.D. Journaling was popular during the Renaissance and in early Japan. As early as the 10th century, the women of the Japanese court kept personal images, dreams, thoughts and poetry in books called pillow books (because they were kept in the bedroom).

Journals were also important to travelers of all kinds. They were used to record details of a journey, places explored, special events, purchases and so on. Journals of sea voyages were vital for recording an official log of activities and command decisions as well as insights and observations that might be useful to other ship captains.

The first person given credit for using what we call a diary was Samuel Pepys. A naval administrator and Member of Parliament, Pepys kept a diary from 1660-1669 that has given historians a truly fascinating and intimate record of what life was like during the English Restoration period. The 19th and 20th centuries saw a continued rise in the number of journals kept and published.

Today, we still use journals to record our personal thoughts and feelings. Journals have become powerful tools for personal psychotherapy, for recording research notes, keeping track of dreams, brainstorming and mind mapping activities, recording recipes, personal ceremonies, and jotting down snippets of writing to be utilized at a later time.

I started making my own personalized journals when I was in college and it is something I continue to enjoy today. There just seems to be something about writing in a book that I have created myself that I find very appealing and energizing. Creating your own journal does require some effort but it is really worth the time and energy it takes to have a very special venue for your innermost thoughts and feelings, dreams and private meanderings.

Crafting any book requires patience and attention to careful measurement, cutting, gluing and craftsmanship. Making your own journal is an undertaking, but one well worth the effort. The time and energy you put into your own personal journal adds energy to the way you will use it after it is completed. You can add your own personality to your journal by creating pages with special images or by adding interesting artistic accents or photographs to the cover.

Personal journals also make beautiful gifts. After my friend Diana learned how to handcraft her own personal journal she made some exquisite ones for her close friends for Christmas gifts. Diana spent time using her computer to add small digital images to the edges and corners of journal pages that would be pleasing to each person she was making a journal for. The thought and effort she put into decorating each page and adorning the covers left those who received them near speechless with surprise and appreciation for her love and attention to crafting something especially for them.

When making a journal for yourself or for someone special, be open to your intuition to help guide you in your choices of fabric, paper, images and cover embellishments and you will create a meaningful and beautiful journal that will be treasured for a lifetime.

Making Your Own Secret Journal

You will need:

- Heavy illustration board for cover
- Paper for your book pages
- Fabric to cover your book
- Cheesecloth
- Interesting heavy paper for inside covers
- Ribbon, cord or metal photo album screws
- Adhesive spray
- Fabric glue, E 6000 or Household Goop adhesive glue
- Printmaking roller or rolling pin
- Fingernail file or small square of fine sand paper
- Pencil
- Chalk (if you have dark fabric for your cover)
- Ruler with metal edge
- X-acto knife or retractable box knife with a good sharp blade
- Scissors
- Leather punch or heavy-duty paper punch
- Decorations for the front cover
- Newspaper
- Paper towels and a damp cloth for wiping away glue from book and fingers

- A flat surface upon which to work (be sure to protect it, especially when cutting with an exacto knife or box cutter – layered cardboard sheets are great for this)

1. Choose the size of the paper you wish to use for your book. Once you have decided on the size you can then measure the heavy illustration board for the front and back covers. Mark out two cover pieces that are 1/2" (12,5 mm) longer than the height of the inner pages and 3/8" (10 mm) wider than the width of the inner pages (the cover width is 1/8" wider due to the 1/8" (3 mm) gap you will create between the cover and attachment strip so that the book will open correctly). Use two to three thicknesses of cardboard as a cutting mat to protect your work surface. Carefully cut your covers with a ruler and a sharp cutting tool such as an X-acto knife. Use a fingernail file or fine sandpaper to lightly smooth any rough edges.

2. Measure a section 7/8" (22 mm) wide along one side of the top cover and along the corresponding side of the bottom cover. Cut these two narrow attachment strips away carefully as you will need them for construction. Set the narrow sections you just cut next to the larger pieces that you cut them from. Mark them lightly in pencil so you will be able to match them up again. Do this for the top cover and the bottom cover. Lightly smooth any rough edges with the sand paper or fingernail file.

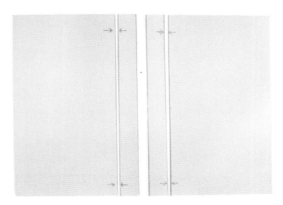

3. Lay out your fabric with the right side turned towards the table. Then place your cover pieces on the fabric. Be sure to lay out each cover piece and attachment strip so that there is a 1/8" (3 mm) gap between them. Also, make sure

that you lay out the other cover in exactly the opposite manner so that they will both match up when covered. Mark a 1" (25 mm) border all the way around the edge of the cover areas. If the fabric is dark use a bit of chalk to draw the edges. Before you pick up your cover pieces use the marker or chalk to mark the corners so you will know where to place them during the gluing process. Carefully cut out the two pieces of fabric and lay them out with the right side facing the table and the wrong side with the corner marks facing up.

4. On a piece of newspaper, in a well-ventilated area, lay out the cover pieces and attachment strips. Be sure that the sides that will make contact with the fabric are turned up, and spray lightly with spray adhesive (if you spray too heavily the adhesive will bleed through your fabric). Then use the markings you made on the insides of the fabric pieces to help you position the sticky sides of the covers and attachment strips on the fabric. Use the printmaking roller or rolling pin to roll across the cover pieces to help them adhere to the fabric. Then carefully flip them over and roll the fabric side. Allow the glue to set for several minutes before moving on to the next step.

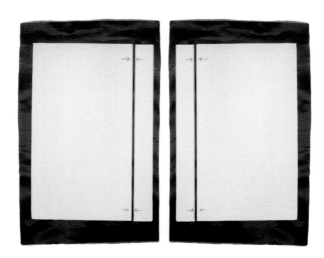

5. Spread a thin layer of fabric glue on either side of the cover next to the 1/8" (3 mm) gap and allow them to become tacky before laying down a 1" (25 mm) wide piece of cheesecloth that will help support the inner cover. Allow to dry while you finish turning under the edges of your book covers (step 6).

6. Lightly spread some fabric glue or silicone sealer (E6000 or Household Goop) on the corners of the fabric. Let them sit for a few moments until they become tacky and then fold them over on to the cover. Use the roller to flatten them to the covers. Allow the corners to dry for several minutes.

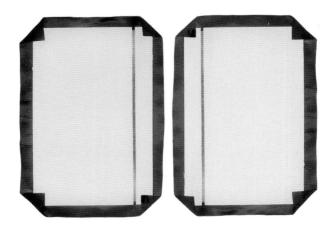

7. Next, spread glue on the fabric around the top, bottom and sides of the covers. Let it sit until it is tacky and then fold the sides and the top and bottom edges over on to the covers. Use the roller to press them down and, if necessary, weight them down with heavy objects to ensure the edges set properly.

8. Choose a fairly heavy or decorative paper to line the insides of your book covers. Measure your inner covers so that a 1/4" (6 mm) border of the book fabric will show around the outer edges after the paper is glued down. Cut or fold and tear the lining papers and check to be sure that the edges are straight (if you tear be sure to crease the paper back and forth several times before tearing). Place the lining pages on the insides of the covers so that the edges are all equidistant from the edges of the inside book covers. Then make a very light mark on each corner of the inside of the book cover to help you place the paper in the correct position after the glue has been applied. On newspaper, in a well-ventilated area, lightly spray the undersides of the front and back lining papers with spray adhesive. Place the sticky sides of the liners on the inner book covers, using the marks as guides. Then use the roller or rolling pin to flatten the paper against the cover and fabric. If you have time you may wish to lay the covers out and place heavy books on them for 20 to 30 minutes.

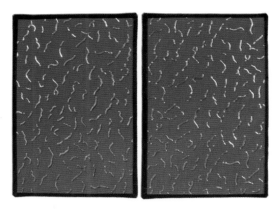

9. In order to set the holes in the attachment strips of the book covers you will need to place a sheet of your paper on top of the book with the holes positioned over the attachment strip. Mark the holes with pencil or chalk and then use a heavy-duty hole punch or leather punch to make the holes through the fabric and cardboard of each cover. Place paper between the covers, lining up the holes with the holes on the attachment strips. Thread ribbon through the holes and tie the ends together or use photo album screws to affix the paper between the two covers.

10. Use adhesive glue (E6000 or Household Goop) to add decorative embellishments as desired, being careful to avoid placing them over the area where the cover bends open.

Now that you have completed your secret journal you should take a few moments to sit quietly with it and imagine how you will use it in the future. See yourself writing in it and opening it to read things that you have written. Allow yourself to enjoy the feeling of satisfaction that you created this personal journal with your own hands for your own purposes. Congratulate yourself on a job well done.

CHAPTER 20

Pouches and Bags

PEOPLE HAVE BEEN using pouches and bags to carry foodstuffs, tools and other valuable items since the times of the early hunter/gatherers. Pouches were often smaller bags that were used almost like pockets, which tended to contain small tools, toilet articles, sewing supplies, or sacred magical items. Because of their more personal nature, pouches were often decorated, sometimes quite intricately. Bags tended to be larger and less decorative than pouches. They were used to carry a number of pouches or to carry other larger items, and often they were tied together, to be carried over the shoulder or on the back of a horse.

Bags and pouches were usually made of materials such as tanned leather or furs, stomachs and bladders of larger animals, bark, woven animal and human hair, grass or fabrics. Pouches frequently included a flap or a small drawstring made of rawhide, sinew or twisted cord. They were originally carried in a larger

bag over the shoulder, but eventually people began to fasten them to a belt or girdle. Ancient armies were known to use girdles with pouches to carry their daggers and eating utensils as well as other items.

Early Europeans used pouches and bags to carry personal items, goods for sale, or the tools of their trade. The term 'cutpurse' came from the act of moving through groups of people and cutting their purses away from their belts while they were distracted by some activity. Cutpurses and bandits preyed on those travelling with purses attached to a girdle or belt, which made travelling particularly dangerous. Over time people began to use pockets to carry things around but pouches were still useful for protecting and storing important things like jewelry, coins or tarot cards. Pouches lined with dark or black fabric were used to keep negative energies away from tarot cards, pendulums, special jewelry or other magical items. Black satin or velveteen pouches for this purpose are still popular and in use today.

Over time pouches and bags have evolved to include a variety of shapes, sizes and closures, including zippers, snap clasps, magnetic clasps and more. Leather remains popular, but plastics and a plethora of designs and weights of fabrics are also available. Some current bags and pouches are more complicated to make than many of us would choose to attempt. But the simple design of a personal pouch is still popular and people now use them to protect jewelry or sacred items, and carry herbs, stones, tarot cards, runes and more.

You can easily make your own pouches and bags for personal use out of leather, faux suede, velveteen or other fabrics. You can even use a sewing machine if you wish, though hand-stitching adds even more to the energy of the purpose for which you create the pouch or bag. The chapter on magical travel altars has a design template for a bag that is very simple and easy to make. It can be drawn shut to hold items but can also be laid out flat to be used as an altar or casting cloth. The instructions below are for a stitched pouch with drawstring.

Making a Small Personal Pouch or Bag

You will need:

- Faux suede fabric or soft leather at least twice the size of the bag you will cut from it, and preferably dark in color to dispel negative energy
- Scissors
- Ruler

- Needle and matching thread or leather punch, needle and waxed linen ('mock' sinew)
- Pins for fabric
- 2 lengths of satin cord or leather thong (each 4 times the width of the finished bag)

1. Draw the shape and size of the bag you are going to make on a piece of paper, adding 1/2" (12,5 mm) extra along each edge for seams. For example, a 4"x 6" (10 x 15 cm) bag would be cut out as a 5"x 7" (12 x 17 cm) rectangle. Once you have made sure your measurements are correct and you are happy with the shape, cut out your paper pattern.

2. Double your fabric or leather with the right sides facing each other. Lay your pattern on top. If using fabric, use pins to attach the pattern to the fabric. If using leather then draw the outline in light marker or chalk on the wrong side of the leather. Cut out your fabric or leather pieces.

3. If you are going to embroider or bead your bag do it before you complete its assembly.

4. Put the right sides together. Fabric edges may be pinned in place for stitching. Leather may be soft enough to sew with needle and thread. Test on a scrap to see how well this will work. If it is too thick you may need to make a series of small holes through which to stitch the 'mock' sinew.

5. For the fabric bag, begin sewing 1 1/2" (38 mm) below the top of the bag, leaving space for the tubes for the drawstrings. Straight stitch all the way around to the other side, just below the stitching line for the drawstring section. You might want to turn and go back, stitching opposite the stitches you placed in your first round. This will make your bag a bit stronger. For leather stitch all the way around from the top of one side to the top of the other and back again if possible.

6. If you are making the fabric bag turn the side edges in and fold the top over so that the fold is about 1/2" (12,5 mm) past the spot where you began stitching the sides. Pin these areas on both sides of the bag. For the leather bag, mark an even number of holes 1/2" down from the tops of the two pieces, making the marks on the side edges half as far away from the edges as they are from the other marks. This way your holes will be evenly spaced all the way around the bag.

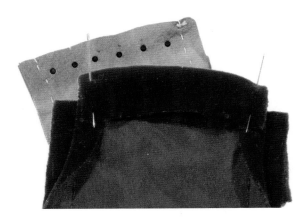

7. For a fabric bag, turn the top of the side edges in and then fold the top down about 1" (25 mm) to the inside and prepare to stitch into place 1/2" down from the top of the fold. This line of stitching should meet up with the end of your side stitching. If not, adjust it so that it does. The tubes you just created will hold your cords when the bag is finished. For the leather bag, use the leather punch to make holes on the marks you made 1/2" down from the tops of the two pieces. You will be putting laces through these holes when the bag is finished.

8. Turn your bag right side out. For fabric bags, attach a small safety pin near the end of the cord of one drawstring and feed it through the tubes you cre-ated on the top of the bag. Tie the ends together. Then do the same from the opposite side of the bag so that you have two drawstrings that when pulled apart will close the bag. Do the same for the other side. For leather do the same thing using the holes you made in the top of the bag.

When your bag is completed, cleanse and clear it with incense, sage smoke or your breath and then spend a few moments with it, imagining it being used in the way you had intended. You now have a personal pouch or bag that you can use for your amulets, wands, runes, crystals and stones, etc.

CHAPTER 21

Magical Tool Chest

WHEN I WAS a little girl I had a cigar box in which I kept my favorite small treasures. Sometimes I would pretend that it was a treasure chest from a royal palace and that I was a princess. Sometimes I was a pirate and the box was filled with my ill-gotten booty. As I grew older the boxes and the items that went into them shifted to match my age. Now I have several magical tool chests. One is for my most prized crystals and stones, another for all of my favorite herbs, and one for my prayer beads, wands and other "extra special" items.

Boxes and chests have been used to store items for centuries and before that people used leather skins. There are safe deposit boxes at the bank, jewelry boxes, packing boxes, shoe boxes, knife boxes, Bible boxes, hat boxes, wine boxes, equipment boxes and decorative boxes, just to name a few.

Most everyone is familiar with stories of pirate treasure and buried wooden sea chests filled with glittering gems, jewelry and gold coins. In the Wild West, Wells Fargo transported money overland in strong boxes on guarded stage-coaches. There's the legendary Pandora's Box of Greek mythology, from which all evil and hope was released. And probably one of the most famous boxes in history is the ancient Ark of the Covenant (as seen in the movie "Indiana Jones and the Raiders of the Lost Ark"). It was a sacred box, which God commanded to be constructed of acacia wood, plated with pure gold, and reputed to carry the first stone tablets of the Ten Commandments.

While you may not be able to make a box plated with gold, you can fashion a personal box using elements that you find especially meaningful. Your secret box can be made out of any material or any small box you like, but in order to imbue it with your own magical essence, it must be decorated specially by you. It is intended to provide you with a secret sacred space that is for your eyes only. Inside this box you may wish to place several small personal items that you can use for creating intent during manifesting activities.

Ideally, your magical tool chest should be at least the size of a small cigar box. However, your choice of box will be dictated by the size of the items you wish to store in it. Craft stores sometimes carry wooden and cardboard boxes of varying sizes and shapes with hinged lids or fitted tops. Hat boxes as well as antique travel and make-up cases also make very interesting bases upon which to build a magical tool chest. How you decorate it is totally up to you. Just make sure that the decoration reflects your own unique personality.

Making a Magical Tool Chest

You will need:

- A box or container of your choice
- Pictures, paints, markers, jewelry items, fabric and/or decorations
- Super glue, E6000 or Household Goop
- Spray adhesive to help attach the lining of the inside of the box
- Fabric or paper for interior lining
- Scotch tape
- Protective newspaper or plastic

1. Make sure that all of the surfaces of your box, inside and out, are clean and dry.

2. Measure the interior of the bottom of your box as well as the height of the sides of the box. Use your ruler to measure the lining fabric or paper to create a rectangle or square with tabs for the sides sticking out in all four directions. If your box is a round box cut a circle for the bottom and a band to fit along the inside edges.

3. Spray the interior of the box with the adhesive and allow it to set for a minute. Carefully place your lining inside and smooth it into place on the bottom and sides. This part can be a bit ticklish with a square or rectangular box. Fold the edges of your lining inwards when you lay it into the box to allow you to adhere the bottom lining first and then carefully work each side up from the bottom edge. Cut off any excess before you press the top edge down.

4. Lay your decorations out on a flat surface, and then organize them in the way that they will be placed on the box.

5. Start attaching your decorations to the box. Spray adhesive is really great for attaching larger paper and images, or fabric. Be sure to spray lightly, in a well-ventilated area, and on protective paper or plastic. E6000 or Household Goop

is wonderful for attaching feathers, buttons, and jewelry bits. You may have to hold some elements in place with scotch tape while the glue sets. Continue to add elements until you are satisfied with the exterior of your box.

When all of the work on your magical tool chest is completed and all of the glue is dry, you can begin to fill it with items that are important to you.

The items you place inside your secret box may include tools you have created for manifesting, such as a set of prayer beads, favorite amulets, wands, runes, or maybe your travel altar. It can also hold personal power items as simple as a lock of your own hair, a special photograph, a bit of nature collected on a walk or a symbol that represents something important to you. Items such as these provide mental and emotional triggers that boost the power of your intent and focus. You can even store favorite essential oils, elixirs and herbs in your magical tool chest if you have room. Or you can make a second one just for this purpose.

By putting in time and effort to decorate and fill your magical tool chest you are bestowing upon it strong manifesting energy that will keep on building as you continue to use and then store your own sacred and magical items in it. You may even find that when you are away from your magical tool chest you can still access its energy with your mind when you need it, even over great distances. All you have to do is close your eyes, take a few deep breaths and imagine that you are opening the lid and using whatever tool you would choose if you had the box in your hands. This is a potent way to use the energy of the items in your magical tool chest at any time, anywhere.

CHAPTER 22

Keys and Charts

FOR MILLENNIA individuals have been consulting sacred texts, seeking the advice of wise ones and searching for ways to expand the power of their magic and their ability to attract wealth, health, love, luck into their lives. When I first started working with crafts as a means of manifesting I deliberately intensified the power of my creations by utilizing moon phases, special symbols, magical and celestial alphabets. As you can imagine, I ended up with quite a lot of books on herbs, crystals, sacred symbols, astrology, and the like. While I enjoyed reading these books, and they all proved very helpful, I found that consulting them could be rather time consuming, and occasionally even a bit boring.

Eventually I decided to compile my own tables and charts of magical elements, using keywords, rather than long descriptions, so that I could gather the information I needed to empower a craft quickly and easily. My keyword lists and my element, zodiac, moon phase tables and magical alphabets have been so useful that I always keep them at hand when I begin to work on a creative project. In fact, I have enjoyed using them so much that I wanted to share them with you, so that you too can quickly access the same simple yet incredibly potent information when you work with the crafts in this book.

Where you discover an area of special interest to you, you will find that there are many great books available to further your own research. In the meantime, please feel free to use the keys and illustrations in this chapter as a guide and add to them your own magical knowledge and information to help you attract all the wonders and joys that life has to offer.

Zodiac Symbols and Properties

ARIES

Mar 21-Apr 20

Ruled by Mars

–

+ Enthusiasm, action,
pioneering spirit, straightforward
– Agressive, impatient

TAURUS

Apr 21-May 21

Ruled by Venus

–

+ Stable, secure, sensual,
reliable, dependable
– Complacent, dogmatic,
inflexible

GEMINI

May 22-Jun 21

Ruled by Mercury

–

+ Communicative, eager,
versatile, fountain of ideas
– Scattered, fickle,
oversensitive

CANCER

Jun 22-Jul 23

Ruled by Moon

–

+ Emotionally connected, caring,
nurturing, family oriented
– Oversensitive, moody, bossy

LEO

Jul 24-Aug 23

Ruled by Sun

–

+ Playful, creative, expressinve,
possesses great will power
– Demanding, intolerant

VIRGO

Aug 24-Sept 23

Ruled by Mercury

–

+ Practical, organized problem
solver, service oriented
– Inflexible, fault-finding,
nit-picky

LIBRA

Sep 24-Oct 23

Ruled by Venus

–

+ Cooperative, communicative,
fair, loves harmony and balance
– Indecisive, insincere, vain

SCORPIO

Oct 24-Nov 22

Ruled by Pluto

–

+ Passion, intensity, power,
transforming
– Manipulative, vengeful,
grudging

SAGITTARIUS

Nov 22-Dec 22

Ruled by Jupiter

–

+ Adventurous, traveler, explorer,
philosophical,educator
– Blunt, excessive,
non-committal

CAPRICORN

Dec 23-Jan 20

Ruled by Saturn

–

+ Patient, determined, high
achiever, organized, structured
– Over-ambitious, rigid,
calculating

AQUARIUS

Jan 21-Feb 19

Ruled by Uranus

–

+ Free-thinking, humanitarian,
revolutionary ideas
– Aloof, self-serving

PISCES

Feb 20-Mar 20

Ruled by Neptune

–

+ Intuitive, compassionate,
giving, universal, creative
– Overfunctioning, impractical,
prone to addiction

Planetary Symbols and Properties

MOON

–

Reflection, feelings,
receiving, fluctuation,
rhythms and cycles

MERCURY

–

Thinking, communication
logic, reason

VENUS

–

Balance, harmony,
relationships (all),
environmental relations

SUN

–

Creation, rulership,
vitality, resurrection

MARS

–

Action, aggression, desire,
energy, how one deals with anger,
meeting needs

JUPITER

–

Confidence, vitality, success,
optimism, generosity,
growth and change

SATURN

–

Responsibility, self-respect,
self-discipline, duty,
limitation, authority

URANUS

–

Invention, originality,
unexpected change, questions
and challenges, revolution

PLUTO

–

Death, renewal, challenges,
transformation, setbacks

NEPTUNE

–

The unknown, illusion,
dreams, ideals,
mysticism, addiction

Moon Phase Symbols and Properties

NEW MOON
(Day 0)
–
Self improvement, romance,
gardening, career

WANING CRESCENT
(Day 26)
–
Self-reflection, letting go,
serving justice

WAXING CRESCENT
(Day 4)
–
Business, changes,
emotions, animal needs

LAST HALF
(Day 22)
–
Banishing illness, negativity
or addictions

FIRST HALF
(Day 7)
–
Love, success, health, courage,
wealth, friendship

WANING GIBBOUS
(Day 18)
–
decisions, emotions,
divorce, addictions

FULL MOON
(Day 14)
–
Manifestation, divination,
protection, money, legal issues

WAXING GIBBOUS
(Day 10)
–
Patience, energy building
for full moon

Day/Planet/Metal Symbols and Properties

MOON
(Silver)
MONDAY
(Moon Day)
–
Reflection, feelings,
receiving, cycles

MARS
(Iron)
TUESDAY
(Tiws Day)
–
Action, aggression,
energy,

JUPITER
(Tin)
THURSDAY
(Thor's Day)
–
Confidence, optimism,
success, generosity

MERCURY
(Mercury)
WEDNESDAY
(Wodin's Day)
–
Thinking, communication,
reason, logic

VENUS
(Copper)
FRIDAY
(Freya's Day)
–
Balance, harmony,
relationships

SUN
(Gold)
SUNDAY
(Sun Day)
–
Creation, vitality,
resurrection

SATURN
(Lead)
SATURDAY
(Saturn Day)
–
Duty, limitation,
authority

148

Elemental Symbols and Properties

EARTH

(North)

–

Physical, steady progress,
fertility, abundance, prosperity.

–

(Taurus, Virgo, Capricorn)

WATER

(West)

–

Flow, spirituality, intuition,
purification, transformation,
abundance.

–

(Cancer, Scorpio, Pisces)

SPIRIT

(All)

–

The coming together of all
elements, all that is, infinite
possibility.

–

(All Signs)

AIR

(East)

–

Ethers, communication, clarity,
spiritual connection.

–

(Gemini, Libra, Aquarius)

FIRE

(South)

–

Clarity, emotion, passion,
purification, power.

–

(Aries, Leo, Sagittarius)

Numerological Properties

0   ALL, infinite possibility, formless, empty yet whole

1   Individual, will, determination, initiates action

2   Balance, receiving, cooperation, understanding, adaptable

3   Interaction, self-expression, creativity, optimism

4   Order, practicality, creation, breaking past limitations

5   Action, expansiveness, exploration, resourcefulness

6   Reactive, responsible, artistic, nurturing, balanced, humanitarian

7   Analytical, seeking, inventive, meditating, peaceful, perfectionist

8   Power, sacrifice, authority, sound judgment, decision making

9   Completion, selfless, self-expression, giving, congenial

11   Highly spiritual, peace and understanding, spiritual knowledge

22   Higher creation, expansion of boundaries, higher order

Color Properties

Red Fire energy, strength, power, good health, courage, passion, protection

Pink Friendship, honor, love, compassion, relaxation

Orange Strength, attraction, luck, encouragement, vitality, physical and metaphysical energy

Yellow Air energy, divination, prosperity, harmony, creativity, confidence, communication

Brown Endurance, steadfastness, protection of the home and objects, improvement of animal health

Green Earth energy, luck, fertility, balance and harmony, healing, prosperity, courage, fairy energy

Blue Water energy, health, intuition, psychic power, patience, tranquility, change, protection, dreams, protection against depression

Purple Power, spiritual development, intuition, ambition, healing, progress, business, spiritual communication, protection, occult wisdom, meditation

Black Ward-off negativity, banishing, universal possibility, protection, truth, spirit contact

Gray Cancellation, neutrality, travel between the veils, veiling of information of intent, vision quest

White Full moon energy, protection, truth, purity, peace, sincerity, meditation, justice, freedom from fear

Silver Lunar energy, success, balance, introspection, psychic development, meditation

Gold Solar energy, power, success, achievement, healing energy, intuition, divination, good fortune

Tree Properties

Alder	Spirituality, inner voice, resurrection
Ash	Protection, knowledge, power, prosperity, healing
Aspen	Eloquence, useful for spoken spell work
Birch	Birth, new beginnings, creativity, purity
Cedar	Protection, love, prosperity
Ebony	Potent and powerful
Elder	Completion, clearing, banishing, prosperity, healing
Grape Vine	Intuition, psychic reception, inspiration, prosperity
Hawthorn	Peace, fertility, restraint, destruction, sexuality
Hazel	Manifesting, protection, wisdom, fertility
Holly	Prophecy, protection, sexuality, animal magic
Ivy	Protection, healing, unity and cooperation
Mahogany	Strong protection
Maple	Longevity
Oak	Optimism, endurance, victory, fidelity, masculine magic
Poplar	Attraction, wealth
Redwood	Protection, love, success
Reed	Fertility, love, family, protection
Rosewood	Love, devotion
Rowan	Empowerment, healing, divination
Willow	Romantic love, fertility, healing, protection, feminine magic

Herb Properties

Ash	Strong protection, cleansing, redirection of energy
Alfalfa	Financial success
Allspice	Luck, success, ideas
Angelica	Protection, blessing, banishing
Anise	High psychic attunement, protection for astral travel, protect from nightmares
Apple/Apple Blossoms	Peace, contentment, love, fertility
Bay Leaf	Protection, inspiration, banishing
Bayberry	Attraction, money, prosperity
Basil	Money, luck, happiness
Benzoin	Purification, communication, amplification
Bergamot	Prosperity, luck, protection
Betony	Banishing negative energy
Borage	Courage, honesty, strength.
Calendula	Dreams, money, healing
Caraway Seeds	Protection of health, memory improvement
Carnation	Protection
Camphor	Cleansing and clearing, banishing, psychic attunement
Cardamom	Love, romance
Cedar	Psychic attunement, third-eye opening, protection
Chamomile	Good luck, prosperity, calmness, strength
Cinnamon	Money, love, cleansing and healing

Herb Properties

Cinquefoil	Money, attraction
Clove	Power, strength
Coriander	Love, protection, relationships
Cumin	Peace, tranquility, calming
Dill	Love, protection
Dragon's Blood	Power, protection
Elder	Protection
Elecampane	Love
Elm bark	Protection against gossip or slander
Eucalyptus	Physical healing and protection, purification
Eyebright	Clairvoyance, fairy vision
Fennel	Change
Fenugreek	Luck, success
Foxglove	Honesty, encourages truthfulness
Frankincense	Male energy, protection, prosperity
Geranium	Protection, love, removes negativity
Ginger	Passion
Hawthorn	Banishing, protection, purification
Hazel	Protection, reconciliation
Honeysuckle	Confidence, prosperity, attraction, clairvoyance
Hyssop	Blessing, purification

Herb Properties

Irish moss	Security, prosperity, success
Jasmine	Seduction, meditation, dreams
Juniper Berries	Luck, success, good fortune
Lavender	Cleansing, calming, protection
Lemon Verbena	Good luck, protection, cleansing
Lemon Grass	Psychic enhancement, meditation, calming
Lilac	Peace, harmony, past life recall.
Lotus	Psychic communication and understanding
Marjoram	Protection, love, friendship, house blessing
Mint	Prosperity, money, psychic attunement
Motherwort	Protection
Mugwort	Clairvoyance, spirit communication, manifesting
Mullein	Courage, release, closure
Myrrh	Female energy, fertility, luck, protection
Orange or Orange Blossoms	Attraction
Patchouli	Manifestation, money
Pennyroyal	Balance, harmony, cleansing, protection
Pine	Cleansing, protective, prosperity
Poppy Seeds	Fertility, prosperity, clairvoyance, intuition
Rose	Love of all kinds

Herb Properties

Rose Geranium	Blessing, luck
Rosemary	Binding, visions and dreaming, improve memory
Rue	Refocusing, protection against negativity
Sandalwood	Clairvoyance, protection, cleansing, healing
Slippery Elm	Protection against gossip
Snakeroot	Banishing herb
St. John's Wort	Protection, removal of negativity, resolve arguments
Solomon's Seal	Luck, wisdom, intuition
Sweet Pea	Attract friendship or romantic love
Thyme	Positivity, courage, protection against negativity
Vanilla	Love, money, seduction
Violet	Truth, encourages honest interactions

Crystal and Mineral Properties

Agate	Grounding, and balance, longevity, protection
Amazonite	Personal power, centering, faith, compassion
Amber	Manifestation and good luck, love, sensuality
Amethyst	Metamorphosis, cleansing, transformation, protection, treat addiction
Apache Tears	Forgiveness, removal of self-limiting beliefs, remove toxins
Apophyllite	Light and love, psychic communication, intuitive vision
Aquamarine	Courage, psychic development, chakra alignment
Aventurine	Heart healing, leadership, loving protection, lung and adrenal healing
Azurite	Divination, subconscious access, visionary attunement, throat, spleen, spine
Black Tourmaline	Protection, removal of negative energy, banishment
Bloodstone	Courage, vitality, strength, honesty, integrity, eyes, lungs, heart, blood
Boji Stones	Healing, balance, rejuvenation of body and mind
Calcite	Energy field amplification, colors work with charkas, pancreas, kidneys, spleen
Carnelian	Ambition, confidence, motivation, asthma, blood pressure
Celestite	Inner peace, harmony, mystical attunement, eyesight, hearing, mental health
Chrysocolla	Peace, strength, prosperity, dispel negativity, diabetes, asthma, leukemia
Chrysoprase	Acceptance, harmony, luck, emotional healing, fertility, eyes, gout

Crystal and Mineral Properties

Citrine	Intuition, personal power, wealth, endurance, digestion, circulation
Coral	Luck, harmony, goals, intuition, guide communication, fertility, arthritis
Danburite	Unity, cooperation, relive depression and anxiety, remove toxins
Diamond	Strength, protection, determination, protection from disease
Dioptase	Abundance, prosperity, nerves, emotional stability, ulcers
Emerald	Prophecy, psychic power, abundance, eyesight, speech, counteract poison
Flourite	Discernment, order, concentration, clarity, purification, viral infections, tumors
Fossil	Business booster, remove self-limiting beliefs, thymus, skeletal system
Galena	Peace, harmony, remove self-limiting beliefs, vascular system, skin
Garnet	Good luck, creativity, devotion, regeneration, depression, anemia, toxin remover
Gold	Master healer, connection to Divine Light, third eye and crown, purifies physical
Hematite	Clarity, balance, reason, memory, transforms negativity, tumors, anemia
Howlite	Emotional balance, calmness, honesty, enthusiasm, dissolve fear and rage
Iron	Mental and emotional balance, diplomacy, personal growth
Jade	Unconditional love, clarity, modesty, courage wisdom, color to chakra healing

Crystal and Mineral Properties

Jasper	Grounding, rejuvenation, protection, sacred practice, astral travel
Kunzite	Full body purification, unity, head/heart alignment, inner freedom, heart healing
Kyanite	High vibrational attunement, mind/matter bridge, meditation, glandular function
Labradorite	Aura protection, psychic, reduce stress and anxiety, digestion, metabolism
Lapis Lazuli	Psychic enhancement, perfection, awareness, integrity, immune system
Lepidolite	Nurturing, relaxation, calmness, clears old behaviors, sore muscles
Malachite	Transformation, clarity, intuition, powerful healing of illness and disease
Mica	Mental flexibility, shamanic journey, grid stone
Moldavite	Transformation, ascension, illumination, channels healing energy
Moonstone	Love, support, intuition, manifestation, fertility, regeneration, reduce pain
Obsidian	Grounding, seeing and releasing old issues, protection
Onyx	Self-mastery, meditation, dreaming, glaucoma, epilepsy, cellular regeneration
Opal	Visions, inspiration, psychic power, clairvoyance, eyesight, metabolism
Paua Shell	Magic, truth, clarity, focus, decision making, bones, spine, nervous system
Peridot	Protection from negativity, physical balancing, ulcers, thyroid, infections

Crystal and Mineral Properties

Petrified Wood	Serenity, grounding, balance, past life recall, bones, spine, hearing
Pyrite	Protection from negativity, improve health, vitality, memory, lungs, cells, genes
Quartz	Universal amplifier of energy, empowerment, psychic aid, purification of body
Rhodochrosite	Love, equilibrium, Earth awareness and healing, conscience
Rhodonite	Love, service, aspiration, emotional and physical balance, heart, lungs, joints
Rose Quartz	Universal love, emotional healing, angelic energy, protection
Ruby	Beauty, transformation, protection, loyalty, heart, blood cleanser, detoxifier
Rutilated Quartz	Determination, decision making, strength, removal of fear
Sapphire	Protection, wisdom, prophecy, hope, faith, healing and loving energy
Selenite	Universal love, transformation, past/future life access, clears negativity
Silver	Gemstone amplifier, safety in astral travel, clears negative energy
Smoky Quartz	Dissolve negativity, clarity, protection from negativity, mineral balance
Sodalite	Logic, rational thinking, clarity, efficiency, unity, glands, metabolism, insomnia
Sugilite	Self-healing, manifestation, spiritual gifts, confidence, headache, cancer
Tiger eye	Grounding, personal power, psychic ability, prosperity, wounds, eyes, throat

Crystal and Mineral Properties

Topaz
Truth, love, success, manifestation, prosperity, psychic communication, detoxifier

Tourmaline
Clear and stimulate body energy centers, healing, insight, color to chakra

Turquoise
Earth/Sky connection, cleansing, communication, attunement, master healer

Unakite
Emotional balance, re-birthing, release of self-limiting behaviors, childbirth

Zeolite
Earth healing, land restoration, release toxins from body, fight addiction

The Elder Futhark Runes

A **ANSUZ**	B **BERKANO**	D **DAGAZ**	E **EHWAZ**	F **FCHU**	G **GEBO**
–	–	–	–	–	–
Message, insight, inspiration	Birth, fertility, growth	Breakthrough, awakening, awareness	Transportation, movement, change	Possessions earned, wealth, luck	Gift, partnership, exchange

H **HAGALAZ**	I **ISA**	J **JCRA**	K **KAUNA**	L **LAGUZ**	M **MANNAZ**
–	–	–	–	–	–
Wrath of nature, destruction	Challenge, frustration, blockage	Fruitful cycle, peace, happiness	Vision, knowledge, creativity	Flow, healing, psychic power, renewal	Self awareness, intelligence, society

N **NAUTHIZ**	O **OTHALA**	P **PERTHO**	R **RAIDO**	S **SOWILO**	T **TEIWAZ**
–	–	–	–	–	–
Delays, restrictions, resistance	Inheritance, past, group priorities	Feminine, secret, mystery, occult	Journey, transition, change of perspective	Success, luck, honor, health	Honor, justice, leadership, authority

U **URUZ**	V/W **WUNJO**	Z **ALGIZ**	EL **EIHWAZ**	NG **INGWAZ**	TH **THURISAZ**
–	–	–	–	–	–
Strength, potential, energy, speed	Joy, comfort, pleasure, fellowship	Protection, shielding, shelter, defense	Purpose, motivation, enlightenment	Masculine, virtue, strength	Conflict, reaction, destruction

The Enochian Alphabet

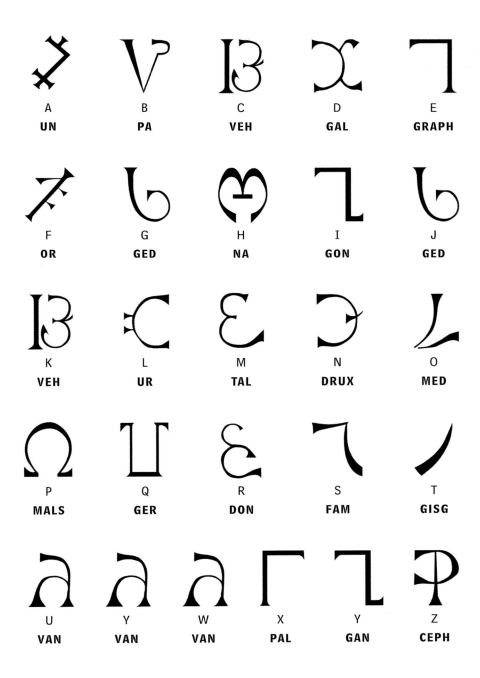

A **UN**	B **PA**	C **VEH**	D **GAL**	E **GRAPH**
F **OR**	G **GED**	H **NA**	I **GON**	J **GED**
K **VEH**	L **UR**	M **TAL**	N **DRUX**	O **MED**
P **MALS**	Q **GER**	R **DON**	S **FAM**	T **GISG**
U **VAN**	Y **VAN**	W **VAN**	X **PAL**	Y **GAN**	Z **CEPH**

The Celestial Alphabet

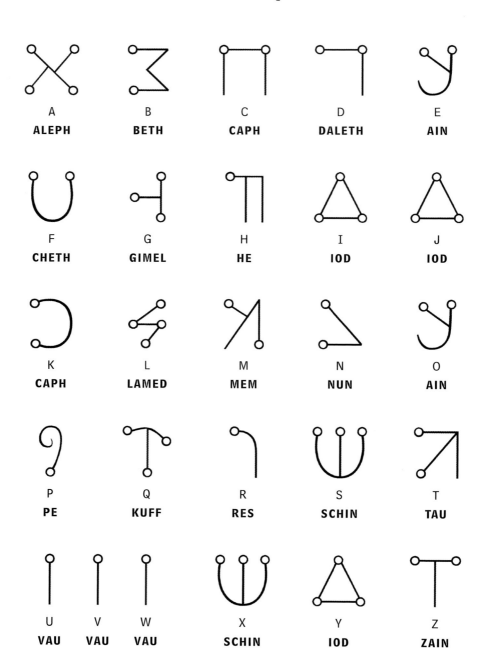

A	B	C	D	E
ALEPH	**BETH**	**CAPH**	**DALETH**	**AIN**
F	G	H	I	J
CHETH	**GIMEL**	**HE**	**IOD**	**IOD**
K	L	M	N	O
CAPH	**LAMED**	**MEM**	**NUN**	**AIN**
P	Q	R	S	T
PE	**KUFF**	**RES**	**SCHIN**	**TAU**

U	V	W	X	Y	Z
VAU	**VAU**	**VAU**	**SCHIN**	**IOD**	**ZAIN**

CHAPTER 23

Recommended Reading

- **Diehn, Gwen**. *The Decorated Journal: Creating Beautifully Expressive Journal Pages*. New York: Lark Books, 2005.

- **Gonzalez-Wippler, Migene**. *Complete Book of Amulets & Talismans* (Llewellyn's Sourcebook Series). St.Paul: Llewellyn Publications, 1991.

- **Greer, John Michael, and Clare Vaughn**. *Pagan Prayer Beads: Magic and Meditation with Pagan Rosaries*. San Francisco: Weiser Books, 2007.

- *"Growing a Witch's Garden - Seeds from Alchemy Works."* Alchemy Works Seeds & Herbs - The Raw Materials of Magick. 19 Jan. 2008 http://www.alchemy-works.com/witchs_garden.html

- **Holaday, Carol**. "PlanetLightworker - December 2002." *Planetlightworker Magazine*, Metaphysics, Spirituality, Non-duality, New Age & Evolution, Lightworkers, Indigo and Crystal Kids. 1 Dec. 2002. 15 June 2008 http://www.planetlightworker.com/articles/joysprite/article14.htm

- **Laszlow, Ervin, and Jude Currivan**. *Cosmos*. Carlsbad: Hay House, 2008.

- **Lipton, Bruce H**. *The Biology of Belief: Unleashing the Power of Consciousness, Matter, & Miracles*. Carlsbad: Hay House, 2008.

- **Lonegren, Sig**. *The Pendulum Kit*. London: Connections Book Publishing Ltd, 2000.

- **Long, Jim**. *Making Herbal Dream Pillows*. Boston, MA: Storey Books, US, 2002.

- **Peschel, Lisa**. *Practical Guide To The Runes: Their Uses in Divination and Magic* (Llewellyn's New Age). St. Paul: Llewellyn Publications, 2002.

- **Rankine, David**. *Crystals: Healing and Folklore*. Milverton: Capall Bann Pub, 2003.

- **Williamson, Marianne**. *Everyday Grace*. Boston: Riverhead Trade, 2004.